DON'T LOOK NOW

21st Century Essays
David Lazar and Patrick Madden, Series Editors

Don't Look Now

Things We Wish We Hadn't Seen

EDITED BY

KRISTEN IVERSEN

AND

DAVID LAZAR

MAD CREEK BOOKS, AN IMPRINT OF
THE OHIO STATE UNIVERSITY PRESS
COLUMBUS

Library of Congress Cataloging-in-Publication Data
Names: Gavazzi, Stephen M., editor. | Staley, David J., 1963– editor.
Title: Fulfilling the 21st century land-grant mission : essays in honor of the Ohio State
    University's sesquicentennial commemoration / edited by Stephen M. Gavazzi,
    David J. Staley.
Other titles: Fulfilling the twenty-first century land-grant mission
Description: Columbus : Trillium, an imprint of The Ohio State University Press,
    2020. | Includes bibliographical references. | Summary: "A collection of essays by
    current and former leaders of The Ohio State University about the contributions
    that OSU continues to make as part of its century land-grant mission"—Provided
    by publisher.
Identifiers: LCCN 2020003834 | ISBN 9780814214442 (cloth) | ISBN 9780814278130
    (ebook)
Subjects: LCSH: Ohio State University. | Education, Higher—Aims and
    objectives—Ohio.
Classification: LCC LD4228 .F85 2020 | DDC 378.771/57—dc23
LC record available at https://lccn.loc.gov/2020003834

Cover design by Christian Fuenfhausen
Text design by Juliet Williams
Type set in Adobe Garamond Pro

Contents

Acknowledgments

The editors wish to thank our contributors, all of whom responded to our prompt with such boldly original essays.

And we also want to joyously mark our intellectual and emotional debt to Daphne du Maurier and Nicholas Roeg.

Preface

I remember reading Daphne du Maurier's collection of stories, *Don't Look Now*, when I was a teenager—the brooding sense of irredeemable loss throughout, with an eerie feeling that an inability to lose grief would only lead to more. What I remember most directly was the very last line of the story: "And I thought to myself, what a bloody silly way to die," when John, the narrator, has been struck in the throat with a knife by the maniacal dwarf he thinks is an endangered child. But the story begins, "Don't look now . . ." as John tries to cheer his grief-stricken wife with the thought that two sisters sitting nearby are trying to hypnotize them. Little does he know.

Little do we know. The perils not only of looking, but of reading—it's been forty-five years since I read *Don't Look Now* and I haven't been able to shake it. Nor have I shaken Nicholas Roeg's brilliant cinematic treatment of the story, the film starring Julie Christie and Donald Sutherland, and, really, Venice. It might as well have been subtitled *Death in Venice II*. It's unnerving and uneasy as few films are, differently from the story, which is first person. Roeg is constantly visually destabilizing us with the authority of his framing and the instability of point of view.

A line that gets repeated throughout *Don't Look Now*: "Seeing is believing." Yes: ironic, sort of. We do believe what we see much of the time. Some of the time we don't want to believe what we see, especially when what we see is unnerving, when it makes us uneasy. Sometimes what we see is distorted by what we want, wish fulfillment, or what we fear, whipped up as a chaser to dreams, or the froth of our repressed death drives. But once we've seen whatever it is that we've seen or think we've seen, like John in *Don't Look Now*, we set something in motion, and that dagger can't be unthrown. The seen can't be unseen.

*

Don't look now, we say. *But.* It's always followed by *but.* Such a complicated set of instructions, no? Yes. Whenever we're told not to do something, we have a natural tendency to want to do it. Don't look. Oh, right. The *but* is the narrative which is seeking some control. As though that might help us survive. Because seeing is sometimes about life and death, memory and language are the governors of our fate.

We have asked a superb group of writers to think and write about things they've seen which they wish they hadn't. That sounds like an invitation to the Uncanny, and for several of the respondents it is. It is also, as you might expect, a series of intense meditations, on what it means to be burdened by being somewhere, being someone, and seeing something. What are the responsibilities therein?

These writers try, at times, to shake off memories like bad dreams. Or: face some images head-on. It's what we all do.

David Lazar

Like all good stories, this one begins in a bar.

I first visited Paris in the spring of 1985. I was working as a stringer for an American newspaper, but what I wanted to do was write—to *really* write—and that meant novels and books and big subjects, not two-column newspaper clips. Armed with a copy of *A Moveable Feast,* I went to every bar and café that Hemingway, Fitzgerald, Stein, or any other American writer with the vaguest whiff of fame might have visited. I sat alone at a tiny table at Les Deux Magots, ordered a scotch, and took out my notebook. I hoped someone might look over and think I was a writer. Or maybe I would feel like a writer. Something. Anything.

Of course, no one paid me the slightest bit of attention. It was mostly tourists, anyway. The strongest feeling I remember from that evening was that it's not a great idea to drink too much scotch.

Hemingway had Les Deux Magots and Tennessee Williams had the Carousel Bar, but in Cincinnati we have Taft's Ale House, which is where David Lazar and I met for a beer in March of 2018 and stumbled upon the idea for this book. There was a literary vibe of sorts. Built in 1850, in a previous incarnation Taft's Ale House had been St. Paul's Evangelical Church, the oldest Protestant parish in the city. The doctrine had changed, but the place still has a strong following, perhaps even more than before, and as we sat in the half-light filtering through the stained-glass windows, we sipped our beers and talked about storytelling. Some of the stories we shared were, as the most important stories are, dark. David had written a beautiful essay about suicide; I had just learned of the suicide of my former husband. We talked about how one lives, or tries to live, with grief and violence and anger, and how those images can burn forever in one's mind. *The seen can't be unseen.*

My own religious upbringing is foggy at best, but I recall my mother talking about the words of St. Paul. God will not give us anything we cannot bear, she said, and he always gives us strength to endure it. She herself had seen many things she wished she hadn't seen. I'm not sure I believed her words then, and I'm not sure I believe them now. But I do know that the telling of stories, in words as powerful as the words that are printed in this book, help us bear the fears and darkness we all face. Things are not what they seem. Life is not what we expect. And yet we endure.

This book is a collection of astonishing writers, taking on topics both searing and revelatory. As you read these pages, I hope you will feel the warm camaraderie of writers at a small bar or café, swapping their stories, sharing their fears, words and images flying around the room. Come, draw up a chair to the table. We've been waiting for you.

Kristen Iversen

My Paradiso

JERICHO PARMS

Beautiful, beautiful. Magnificent desolation.

—Buzz Aldrin, upon joining Neil Armstrong on the moon

I am thinking of shapes, how the snake and curve of a line becomes a figure eight, becomes two rings joined, everlasting, never-ending. I am thinking of the letter *S* and how it is nearly one infinite chain. Nearly, but not. On my inner wrist there is a scar—one I've had since girlhood—that looks like something written in sand and partially blown away. I want to conjure the tides, but I am so far from the ocean as I write that memory spirals away from me. Perhaps whatever follows in these lines I owe to that distance. And to the swimmers and oceanographers, scientists and shore divers, mariners and mystics, artists, biologists, storm chasers, and foragers who face the erosion of beauty every day, the alchemy of memory— the elusive reel none of us can control. If scars serve as a lighthouse to the past, how do we determine the future? If only memory could expose the path ahead. If only we could receive signals from the moon.

*

In the 1988 film *Cinema Paradiso,* written and directed by Giuseppe Tornatore, set against the backdrop of an Italian village just after World War II, a young Salvador di Vita, along with other townspeople, escapes dark postwar realities by frequenting the village movie theater. The local priest, acting as the moral censor, is ever-present, ensuring nothing untoward appears on screen during the films, which he has already screened, demanding that all kissing scenes be edited out prior to their premiere. In Tornatore's film, Salvatore befriends a projectionist, Alfredo, who takes a liking to the mischievous boy, lets him watch movies from the projection booth, and ultimately teaches him how to operate the projector.

✳

I befriended a projectionist, too. During a long winter I found myself broke in a small New England town. I worked the concession stand in a two-screen movie theater on Main Street because it wasn't enough to teach, and because having recently emerged from a few years of depression and anxiety, I wanted the monotony of shift work, show times, a decorated tip jar, and the distraction of a changing marquee. I had just turned thirty; I was in love with a man but characteristically reluctant to define that love as I attempted to navigate the push and pull between freedom, independence, and responsibility to others.

Although nearing seventy, Bill, the theater's main projectionist, has the energy of a young man. He plays tennis when he can, tells stories about his days in the circus, and crams into a small sedan with his friends and heads to the beach. He loves film more than anyone I've known. He grows easily frustrated, in large part because he likes a certain order, timeliness, and takes his work as lead projectionist seriously, as craft. But when a film is on and there is time to kill, he talks on end. Bill routinely pulls from the booth his folding chair and positions himself next to the concession counter in the tiny house lobby. Although he always has a book and his glasses ready, he rarely makes a dent in his reading during our shifts together. Instead we fill the time with stories from our vastly different lives.

Years later, walking the rotunda of New York's Guggenheim Museum—a building that with its monumental spiral design excites my sense of tumbling—my partner and I visit a traveling retrospective of the abstract painter Agnes Martin's work. The exhibition featured the artist's serene, sparse, square paintings composed of signature grids, lines, and horizontal bands of color which carved out her place as one of the few female artists who gained recognition in the male-dominated art world of the 1950s and '60s. We start at the top of the Guggenheim's sloping gallery and work our way down. My partner, an artist, insists that a top-down approach is the only way to view the museum, "so you never tire of the incline." The security guard posted at the top of the spiral confirms that assertion with a stoic but approving nod. Before we turn our attention to the canvases on view, I lean over the inside wall of the museum's rotunda and peer below. The ground-level lobby is full of visitors, tourists milling about like tentacles of anemone or dislodged debris in a tide pool. Among them there are elderly, schoolchildren, and chaperones. Holiday travelers snap photographs. A Japanese tour group follows a docent's raised flag. I see a woman casually rocking a stroller with her foot as she peruses the exhibition catalogue before viewing the show. From my bird's-eye view she strikes me as vaguely familiar, but amid the bustle of a museum Sunday I can't quite determine why.

The thing about the letter *S* that I find so seductive is the negative space it creates. The static start and stop of the line appears as if an invisible thread bound together its ends. Similarly, in good stage productions we never see the cord that holds the woman flying through the air. *Such bold illusion! Such sleight of hand!* I am thinking of the vocations of women. Should I attempt to fly through the air? Should I marry? Have children? Pursue a landing on the moon? My grandmother, in quiet moments, painted landscapes and still lifes. My mother, while pregnant with me, flipped burgers by day and made extra money as a seamstress. She later taught elementary and middle school: art, English, science. I worked in retail, interned in Washington, sold audio tours at a New York art museum, taught college writing courses. Every chance I get I go elsewhere, to try on the term *writer* like a dress I've borrowed from a friend that does or does not fit the curves of my shoulders, hips, and spine.

Before she found painting, Agnes Martin was a swimmer. Although she left her native Saskatchewan when she was young, she recalls the landscape was "so flat you could see the curvature of the earth." Martin grew up in Vancouver, where she swam daily and excelled on her high school swim team. In 1936, when Berlin hosted the Olympic Games, she nearly qualified for the Canadian national team. At the Guggenheim, I walk from one canvas to the next and imagine Martin swimming: the splash of her arms cutting the surface, her body gliding, leaving lines in her wake. I imagine her in the aquamarine lanes of a pool, completing lap after lap, her breath steady as she releases a deliberate exhale with each stroke. Just across the park at the Natural History Museum, a massive model of a blue whale hangs on display, its neck grooved with horizontal lines.

At ninety-four feet and over twenty thousand pounds of fiber-glass, the replica was based on a female whale found off the coast of South America in 1925. Though they've been hunted to near extinction, blue whales are the largest of animals alive today. They have a haunting deep song that can be heard hundreds of miles away, a gentle intelligence, a majesty and patience to them that reminds me of Martin herself. Martin, who never wavered from her own artistic vision, who ultimately sought solitude away from the art scene of New York City.

At the theater, Bill shows me how to work the projector. Two wheels are stacked to form a figure eight, an S fully realized. Bill's hands move steadily, keeping track of all the details. He removes a spool of 35mm film from a flat canister and threads it into the projector. Once loaded, the film moves seamlessly, like the tide. Over the industrial hum, Bill explains the timing of the reels, how years ago, when films came in multiple reels, projectionists used to mark the spools with cigarette burns, cue marks, to signal that the particular reel was nearing its end, that it was time to prepare the next. The marks, while not insignificant, largely went unnoticed, invisible to a viewer's naked eye—a viewer otherwise immersed in a visual experience. "What we don't look for we don't see," Bill says in a professorial tone. As he moves, I search for shapes in the liver spots on his skin.

Another time, Bill leans into the projector, slowing down his movement to show me, yet again, how to thread the film through the feeder. Bill discusses his favorite movies as if they are women, sizing them up by sight and sound, on-screen performance, directing and cinematography. In turn, he talks about women sometimes as if they are less than women. He knows I am on to him, sees the reflexive cringe in my expression when he makes suggestive comments, but chalks it up to a generational divide between us. When spring arrives he watches young women walking outside and feigns a shiver. "I love this time of year," he says. "Everyone starts showing more skin." Without belaboring the point, he turns back to me. We are discussing films based on books and the key to successful adaptation. As he moves, I notice the flecks of calcium like small fossilized shells in his nail bed. I wonder sometimes how the trajectories of our lives would look if we lay them side by side. We could not be more different but there is a gentleness within him—a whale-like tenderness beneath oft-grand gestures—that gives me confidence, steadies me against all of the unanswered questions.

Sometimes during a movie, after I've restocked the concession stand for the late show, I sit inside the booth. Bill is somewhere on his chair thumbing the pages of a hardcover, a historical account of obscure World War II battles. Alone inside the booth, I close my eyes in the dark and listen to the rotation of the wheel, the slow breathing of the projector. On screen Cate Blanchett looks as stunning as ever. Greta Gerwig is making a splash. Jennifer Lawrence woos the world. Inside the booth, the muffled sound of their voices resonates against the rhythm of classic machinery. The light from the projection waxes and wanes with each scene, illuminating the small strips of film, release schedules, festival flyers, and other miscellany tacked on the walls. Peering through the window, I scan the silhouette of the audience, and delight in knowing that hardly a soul knows I'm there. I am inside a lunar body, holding the reins of light and shadow.

✳

At a young age, I learned the power of the tide. Now that I am older, I realize the time I was whisked and spun by the current on the Long Island shore when I was six was a small-scale lesson in water's desire. Which is to say that it could have, had it wanted to, carried me away forever, all the way from the Eastern Seaboard to a port town in Portugal. That is, had the moon complied. Caught in the messy tumble of a wave, I lost control of my body. My head thrashed against the stone floor of the shore. Sand flooded my mouth, my ears, all of my orifices. All I could hear was the full throttle of a machine. I kept wishing, had it been cold enough, and not for the tide, I could have been frozen in the deep churn of an iceberg, caught like a bird in the noose of a six-pack ring, in an island of plastic straws and soda bottles. Preserved on ice, put out of my misery. Instead during moments of uncertainty, the shoreline still flashes into view. I still recall the feeling of tumbling, still feel salt water in my nostrils and lungs, the scratches along the soft flesh of my legs, the way I might have issued a siren call had I the instinct or the gift of echolocation to sense the whirling shore.

During the weekend matinee, children arrive looking for sweets and popcorn. Bill shows them the projector, as if it were a wooly mammoth on display. As they shuffle off into the main theater, Bill turns to me and winks. "You should have some," he says, nodding in the direction of the kids. "They're sticky as all hell, but . . . you should do it." Once the audience is settled in the theater and the movie has begun, I step into the booth where the children have been and look for evidence of their curiosity: fingerprints on the film canisters, a fallen candy wrapper. Looking out over the darkened audience I find the children in fidgeting forms. *Yes,* I think. *Surely this is*

how the moon must feel. Out there, I am a beautiful bride, the mother of a sweet fleshy child who I love without resentment, only kindness, and teach how to sew on a machine like my mother and how to appreciate old movies. Through the ticket window, I see Bill covering my post at the concession stand. He has a way of making things look easy, shrugging simplicity into large, daunting questions as if to say, "Look, all the evidence you need is right here." As he scoops a fresh batch of popcorn, he talks to a young woman whose slender slouch— both inquisitive and insecure—reminds me of a younger self. Over the hum of the projector I hear him say, "It will get better." When the woman has left, Bill joins me in the booth and describes her as a smart but brooding drifter. "I told her things would get better," he says, and then, squinting toward the viewing window, repeats himself: "It will get better."

✳

Opening night of a new movie, I watch a couple in the audience groping in the dark. They fall asleep in the back row of the theater as I clear the house seats of trash. Instead of disturbing them, I let them be, smiling at the thought of them waking in the midst of the second showing, how instead of needing to be anywhere but there, they might groggily snuggle back into each other's arms and watch again. Bill starts up the projector. I hear the familiar click and tacky hum as I take the crumpled bills of two young girls late arriving. They giggle at the boys who have led them here, to the late show, which will release them after midnight into the silent small-town streets. I wonder how many times they have been in this scene, playing the budding female, that adventurous balance between lightheartedly guarded and uninhibited, that role of a lifetime.

✳

At night, I hear the whispering alphabet of my partner's body as I squirm in the dark. I picture the *I* of his pupil faced with blinding light, the *O* of the navel, the *U* like a horseshoe where the base of the throat meets collarbone. *I. O. U.*—and suddenly the body is a debt I owe, or one owed to me. I cannot be sure. Where the leg meets the groin, the crease forms the wings of a *V* and I can't help but think of the word *vow,* that most solemn of promises, to dedicate, to be beholden to. The letter *S,* on the other hand, is more a movement than a thing, more the shape of a beckoning pose than an anatomical location, something like the swaying of hips, the crossing of legs, the gesture of an arm curled around one's neck as we dance in an awkward square before the fireplace listening to the record player sigh in circles. The letter *S* suggests plurality, multiplicity, all things that cannot be pinned down or singled out. The severed lines of the letter *S* open the space of memory, seeking to be rejoined, cauterized like a wound, to play ad infinitum.

"I don't like circles," Agnes Martin once said, "—too expanding." In Martin's paintings the grid is a completely abstract form. "It's not what is seen, it is what is known forever in the mind." Perhaps that is how I feel about the letter *S,* the lines that in their turning, in the abstract space—the in-between—contain memory, trace findings, insight into identities otherwise undefined.

In *Cinema Paradiso,* Salvatore and his friends crave the visual representation of love and lust to soothe their growing bodies. At several points the movie zooms in on the boys whooping and cawing in their seats, whistling and jeering. Each of them their own vision of buckteeth, round cheeks, and over-sized ears. On screen a woman loosens a man's tie and just as they lean in the footage cuts to a new scene, inspiring frustrated howls and heckles from the audience. Their thwarted curiosity is palpable. Their foiled desires are tangible—round, billowed, swelling. All these years later, it's as if they are still there in that small Italian village trying to reclaim what makes them decisively human, animal, alive, and untethered. Maybe I am trying to do the same. Can I be a woman, married? Can I be a mother without redrawing my lines or changing shape?

At the theater one evening, Bill and I discuss a French-German film, starring Marion Cotillard and Matthias Schoenaerts, both of whom I like. In the film Cotillard as Stéphanie loses her legs after an accident involving a whale and finds love with a bare-knuckle boxer. Bill hasn't yet seen the movie. Instead of his usual premature critique, he launches into a monologue about the state of the oceans—how wrong we are to treat the whales the way we do. Bill continues, citing intelligence tests completed on dolphins in the 1970s and trying to contextualize the so-called phenomenon of beached whales. "A farce," he says. A whale knows the limits of the ocean better than we ever will, he tells me. They can sense the nearing presence of the shore. If a whale shows up caught on dry land, it hasn't "lost its bearings," he says. "It's lost its will to go on." He combs the thick white strands of his beard. "I'm talking about suicide, you realize." I nod. I realize.

If it were true, Bill's theory of the whales would exist as facts do in the world, adding to the poetry of phenomenon, giving cadence to the magnificent love affair—not on screen, or in the broken lives of the human heart, but in the epic long poems of the moon and the ocean. If whale suicide were a thing, it would offer a sober retelling of the universe: in which our greatest creatures fall collateral in the ancient affair between earth and sky. Every year, thousands of cetaceans strand on coastlines around the world, and many die. Sometimes they beach alone, but often they are found clustered in rows along the shore. Whales are conscious breathers. Inhalation is deliberate as they rise to the water's surface. Although descendent from land-dwelling creatures, for the now-sea-dwelling mammals, too much exposure to oxygen is fatal. They hyperventilate. They dehydrate. Their mouths unhinge. Their eyes glaze.

When Martin titles one of her five-foot-square paintings *I Love the Whole World* I want to believe it. I want to believe that being submerged does not equate to being invisible, but allows for solitude. Had I known this as a girl tied up in the ocean's tight grasp I may have relaxed my shoulders and found my way to the surface. I want to believe that intellect and inspiration can be equal partners guiding our instinct. Martin lived by herself her whole life and once remarked that "You can't be an artist if you can't be alone." What if one can be alone, but chooses otherwise? Does such a choice endanger solitude or threaten ingenuity? Does some part of oneself suffer obsolescence or worse, battle extinction? A whale beached on the shore has little hope for survival. And yet, do they call out to no one? Would we ever know as they lay stranded on their sides, their one eye staring up at the moon?

*

During a Sunday matinee shift, a man drives two towns over to see a showing of Terrence Malick's latest film. As he takes his ticket, he asks about the state of the 35mm film industry with a genuine weariness, downright distrust of digital technology, and walks away before I respond, shaking his head as he enters the main screen theater. After the movie he loiters in his seat among the last of the viewers to leave. Back in the lobby he appears bleary-eyed as he touts his reverence for the directing, likens it to a spiritual. "None since Bresson—none since Goddard even, have placed such poetry on screen," he says. "Poetry." The movie is the best he's seen since *Days of Heaven* or *Badlands,* which, were one not familiar with Malick's oeuvre, would sound like a mercurial journey between celestial divinity and earthly grit. The man speaks with Bill, who has grown genuinely engaged, their shared cynicism softening the creases around his eyes, his head nodding as if powered by its own force. They discuss the shift from 35mm to digital film. Bill shows him the one remaining projector. Through the ticket window, I watch the men standing side by side before it and hear their voices shift to an awestruck pitch, as if marveling at a spectacle of antiquity or industrial homage. I wonder if they see in it themselves, sense the day when they too will become obsolete, or if they simply marvel at the machine the way visitors to the New York Natural History Museum circle beneath the fiberglass replica of the giant blue whale. When the man leaves, Bill is quiet the rest of the day.

Throughout her roughly forty-year career, Martin painted horizontal bands on 6x6 square canvases. In the last decade of her life, she scaled down her canvas to 5x5. Doing the arithmetic in her head, then on paper, in drawing, then on canvas, she determined how wide each blue band or white line or plane of beige or gray would be. Life is a series of decisions, choices, adjustments that begin when we first learn to take in air, the way we have to learn to hold our breath underwater, to tread and float and measure our strokes in order to not sink from the weight of our bones.

Amid Martin's work in the galleries of the Guggenheim, I keep turning back up the walkway and realize I've been looking for the woman with the stroller—the one I had seen rocking her child with her foot when I looked down the rotunda. I keep wondering if she has made it all the way up, imagining her landing at the top and coming to a rest, the release in her legs like some lack of gravity, the light blues, yellows, whites of Martin's later work issuing some form of breeze or relief. And yet, I both know and don't know how womanhood has no end. It is not an *S* with severed ends. It is not Frank Lloyd Wright's architectural spiral nor the endless planes and horizons of Martin's grids. Perhaps it is circular, even spherical.

There is a small depression in the wall above my bed, which resembles an oversized chicken pox scar. A slight hollow. A dime-sized crater. I like to think it is my own snapshot of the moon. Below it the bed is warm. I can hear my partner next to me resting soundly. I wish, were that small indentation indeed representative of the moon, she would drop her head just so and look at us: the way the moonlight makes rivers look cleaner than they are, makes sheets look like cool waves dancing. Sometimes a splash of bird shit on concrete looks like a teardrop the moon has shed, and I think: What reason does she have to cry? And, really, what reason do I? We all want something to make us swell with strength and certainty about who we are.

A couple years after I stopped working at the theater—still partnered but unmarried, still writing and teaching but juggling fewer side jobs—I received an email from one of Bill's close friends announcing his death. Bill had been ill with pancreatic cancer, stage four. His friend described his last evening as one of good spirits, watching films, listening to the records he loved. The email read, "*Up to the very last, even with increasing fatigue and weakness, Bill was coherent, gracious . . . valiant and kind.*" Having outgrown his spirit and seen his quality of life diminish, his body had abandoned him. "*It's a great sadness, but he died the way he lived—on his own terms.*" I reread the email, focusing on the final phrase—*on his own terms*. We lived in a state that had recently amended its laws regarding patient choice at end of life, or "physician-assisted death," once referred to as "physician-assisted suicide." I nod. I realize. I recognize that unspoken *S*. I imagine Bill, sensing the limits of his life like an approaching shore, reaching out to touch the cool expansive sands, to scrawl something in the surface before it washed away. I imagine the end credits still rolling long after he closed his eyes.

The letter *S* is the only thing standing between *exist* and *exit*. To be, and to leave. I don't believe my body is abandoning me with its steadfast desire to recall memory, but rather may be leading me. Past moments can teach us about ourselves, guide us toward something quiet and steady that may appear ordinary, banal, even, but is rich with a complex interior. If I could splice together all the deleted scenes of memory, I wonder if— despite the reckless indulgence and self-harm, a reluctance to commit—I, too, have truly loved. And, were that story told, framed by the mise-en-scène of nostalgia, would it inspire laughter or tears? Even the tides rock back and forth. Even the moon issues decrees of hysteria. Where one sees sadness in the somber gray of Martin's mid-career works, I feel grounded in their subdued grace, their stillness. The village priest in Tornatore's classic screened films for images of sinful lust, yet such images became the primer for Salvatore's adolescent longing, such censorship became a lesson in quelled passion and desire. We screen our own perspective, looking for faults, any trace of the taboo in the footage of our lives, the landmark moments, and the smallest memories.

Weeks after learning of Bill's death, I browse through old emails I received from him: video clips, mostly, of illustrated shorts with orchestral soundtracks, and other snippets of classic and art house films; the occasional book recommendation, too, or an online article such as the *New York Times* heralding "The End of Courtship." I open one email, titled "bird ballet," and remember him sending it to me shortly after one of our friendly disagreements over gender politics and the media had escalated into an angry debate. The footage captured the mesmerizing sight of hundreds of starlings silhouetted against a dusky sky, swooping in unison, forming vague shapes then dispersing in the air. Watching the aerial acrobatics—which I only later recall is known as a murmuration, often in preparation for roost—it appears like one thousand paper cranes tossed in the air or particles aloft in space. I think how in a matter of months the ground will begin to thaw and with the first signs of spring, young women will be walking along Main Street in tank tops and shorts, loving the way their skin feels in the sun, thankful to have grown out of their skinned knees and one-piece bathing suits, thankful that when they head to the beach they can stand up to the tide without being washed away. I think of whales congregated on shore. I think of the stickiness of children.

In the final scenes of Tornatore's *Cinema Paradiso,* we see Salvatore years later as an adult. Upon learning of the death of his beloved projectionist, he returns to his village to find Alfredo has left him a single reel. As he projects the film, we see him bathed in its cool flickering light, smiling, then laughing as the image before him reveals a dreamlike montage of love scenes and breathy gestures—all of the spliced images that had been censored from view. The many scraps of film had been secreted away, preserved, restored to form a most life-affirming gift.

I was born too late to have memories of the moon landing. But I have read of them: families gathered around the television set, the sense of history infusing the air. I've seen the footage of Neil Armstrong and Buzz Aldrin slow-stepping their way onto an unfamiliar surface, their grainy, flickering figures representing human achievement. I don't envy that voyage. I'm not interested in stepping on the moon, the surface of which Aldrin subsequently described as "moist talcum powder." I would rather sneak into the Guggenheim after hours and bed down below Martin's square canvases: *This Rain. Night Sea. Innocent Living. Contentment.* I would rather search for beached whales along the ocean's edge. If only we could curl up inside the chamber of a whale's heart and pretend as if we had ourselves landed on a moist powdery planet, stepped onto a cloudy surface—perhaps the umpteenth man, perhaps the very first woman. Nonetheless everyone is there. We spread

our fingers through the baleen walls and through each other's
hair and think *how beautiful, how beautiful, this desolation*—
No, let me rewind and begin again: I would rather sit in
the projection booth as Salvatore and his squirming friends
giggle through footage of film-worthy kisses, one image after
the next embedding in their memory, each dramatic embrace
assuring them that there is more out there to crave, infinite
evidence of love—not galaxies away, but here, on earth.

But for the Grace

XU XI

許素細

> When saw we thee a stranger, and took thee
> in? Or naked, and clothed thee?
>
> —Matthew 25:38 (King James)

Let me be blunt: I, too, have courted desperation. It's almost inevitable when we all are just a wee bit mad around the edges, whether or not we're actually bipolar, psychotic, schizophrenic, manic, clinically depressed, ADD, catatonic. Or just plain mad. Our longings are madder, fed by desires that were once un-voiced, un-staged, un-known. The sheep and goats, there's no division now. Three times before the cock crowed, marking the end of my terrible twenties.

By the time I left that terrible time behind, I no longer trusted what I thought I saw, or heard, in those three desperate, desperate pleas.

✳

The first time, a student in my co-ed dorm. He was skinny-tall, this pothead with the Einstein hair. We talked occasionally, intimate strangers as we walked across our cold, cold campus, back when climate was not yet changed. By early October, winter edged out autumn and spring thaw could last till mid-May.

For sure he had a name, but that has vanished into the cesspool of oblivion. We were all oblivious, hippy-happy, because pot was rampantly sweet. It was the early '70s.

Having jumped ahead a semester in credits, I was a tween, no longer a junior but not yet a senior. It was my second year as RA, resident assistant, a job that offered a room of one's own and half the board. The dining hall was more than the horn of plenty. As a foreign student on the F-1 visa, with employment limited to on-campus work, I needed anything to reduce the cost of what was, for my family, an expensive American college education. Even though it wasn't the Ivies, or New York City, or somewhere comparable to my far more cosmopolitan Hong Kong world even before its economic rise. It was long before Asia dared thumb its nose at the West, the way it can now when the West is no longer the promise of tomorrow. Restraint before globalized desire seduced, enlarging our appetites, before greed, and debt, were good.

So there I was upstate in the far east, due north of New York City, at the smallest four-year SUNY, wandering the corridors of Kent Hall, the dorm with a party reputation because it had previously been all male. Compared to the cat fights I broke up during my previous year at the all-female dorm, my current woman's wing was relatively calm, and roommates were not changing as often as underwear. So there I was in Kent, my last year in college, feeling mature enough, at nineteen, to handle the quaintly sexual innuendo of a guy dorm gone gal.

Winter had not yet completely arrived, just as Watergate had not. The unsuitable blond boyfriend had already dumped me and my desperation had moved well past a Dorothy Parker imitation suicide. I even felt slightly superior to my Algonquin heroine, because counseling controlled my emotions sufficiently so that I did not need to try a second time, the way Parker did, also unsuccessfully. We are women, hear us roar, a mere man did not rule our self-worth. Faith in feminism and psychology.

So when a ruckus burst the nighttime silence out in the hallway—I was the RA on duty that evening—I opened my door. A group of guys had forcibly stripped him, that pothead with the Einstein hair, brought him upstairs to the gals' floor, where they dumped him outside my room, right in the middle of the wing. As I opened my door I heard his plea, *No, please, not my underpants.* His captors had raced off as several other doors opened to peer at his cowering nakedness. He met my eyes, *Cover me please.* I grabbed a blanket, threw it over him, shoved him into my room and closed the door. Called his RA, said, Bring clothes. An incident over almost as quickly as it had begun.

But for years I could not un-see, could not un-hear his anguished face, his whimpering plea. A quarter of a century later, I tried to articulate it as fiction in a workshop in San Francisco, and failed. Columbine had not yet happened then and *Mean Girls* was still six years in the future.

Meanwhile, back in the past, life carried on as if nothing had changed. But he no longer met my eyes when we ran into each other. He wanted to avoid me, and we never spoke again after that night.

Spring eventually arrived.

The sky was clear the day he was arrested. This was a more distant ruckus, across campus at the science building, one I rarely entered. As the grapevine buzzed, I thought of him— quiet but intelligent, less the pothead he appeared to be, more the smart but awkward kid who didn't fit in. We had talked a little music and philosophy back when we still spoke. Eventually the facts emerged: He had assembled a bomb to blow up the chemistry lab. How long had he hunted down that information in the library? How slowly and patiently had he found what he needed, at the local hardware store undoubtedly, or perhaps even in the labs at college? Patty Hearst was recently a headline. If you can't lick 'em, join 'em, could that have been his credo? Terrorism begins at home before it explodes on the rest of society.

And the more things change, the more they don't. "Clothe the Naked" is a short story by Dorothy Parker from the 1930s, about a blind black boy who goes forth proudly one day in his new hand-me-down suit his single mother obtains from her rich employers. The laughter and derision he encounters in the street sends him fleeing back home, cowed. There is no redemption.

✳

The second time, a colleague at the airline in Hong Kong. The unsuitable first Scottish husband was already divorced and I had abandoned the rebound Chinese fiancé. The roar of my womanhood equaled "choosing" the men I slept with and dumped, the sting of that first rejection by the blond in college never completely un-stung. It was difficult to recognize my immaturity, though, when hormones and insecurities abounded. *Sex and the City* was still a future non-shock, and *Fear of Flying* the moment's benchmark.

If part of a bee stinger remains unremoved, the body will eventually swallow it up somehow, although the online jury chatter is still out on that score. The medical community says to remove the stinger as soon as possible. However, even they concede that the oft-stung individual can build immunity. Not unlike the sex act, because promiscuity simply inoculates one against heartbreak, or so my terrible twenties were bent on proving. In my books, Erica Jong was a scaredy-pussycat.

Is sex something we actually need if procreation is not the point?

He was Audit, I was Advertising. It was my second to the last year in the job because the call of the wild was growing louder, seducing me away from my promiscuous but boring business world in favor of the writer-in-progress. As an odd Asian female who traveled frequently for work in the region (but was not a flight attendant), I was once again a tween, neither properly female and certainly not male. Company regulations meant I always wore skirts and heels. There was no mistaking my gender although my survival depended on being one of the boys.

It was also a colonial era, when white boys ruled, although the local Chinese boys were beginning to rise, at least in Hong Kong. Nixon had already been to China and it was just before Carter tore down the bamboo curtain. Hong Kong's international airline was a capitalist, for-profit British 行 (or Hong), unlike the nationalized carriers in most Asian nations. Airlines were monopolies. Flying wasn't cheap and the industry still profitable, although that reality was already sliding down slipperier and slipperier slopes of consumer demand. My pay was good, the benefits brilliant, and the Western men roving and roaring around the region succumbed greedily to yellow fever. Few Asian women roared, which meant that those of us who did had our pick of men. As long as love and marriage were off the table, since the majority of rovers were about to be, or were otherwise engaged to one of their own. A tight Asian pussy, I was actually told by more than one Western lover, was my great asset. "Lover" was a kinder, gentler name; many were merely sex partners. It was easy to be heartless in such a world.

Onto my plane hopped the kinder, gentler audit man. He was a local Chinese, a few years older than me, reporting, as I did, to a white man boss. It was only in Operations among the flight attendants and ground staff, or at Customer Service, that Chinese (including some women) were promoted to management. On the business side, Sales had Chinese managers, but all the other departments were headed by British executives, or the odd Australian like my boss. The revolution was still a tea party, which would have made Chairman Mao turn in his grave.

Let me be blunt: He was a hopeless lover. A virgin, clunky, stuck in the local culture that shaped him, having busted ass to get to where he was. With my foreign university degree, English language, and Western cultural fluency, I was more tween than he ever could hope to be, able to hang with the white world as readily as the local one, the way the Chinese university grads on the executive track could, even though I was not one of them. What was the attraction? That he took my position seriously? That he talked to me as an equal? That he would never outrank me, the way I knew the other Chinese executives all would in time, because a woman, even one on the executive track, would never rise as quickly? I knew my pay outstripped his, even though I was a far more recent hire. Life divided us, sexual experience divided us, education divided us, language divided us, class divided us. I lived in my own place, he did not, as most locals lived at home. He had a girlfriend, a good girl, a virgin, for whom he was saving money to marry. I was just the whore.

Except that I wasn't, not really. We became sort-of friends. I took him to the restaurants and places in my privileged Hong Kong world which he did not know how to access. I paid my own way, something that rarely happened on dates back then. And afterwards, even though it became less and less something that felt right to do, I brought him to my bed.

On our last date—I forget where we ate, but it was likely something in my repertoire—he said, *teach me please. Show me how to live in your world and let me be a part of it. I can learn. Take me please.*

His gaze unnerved me. My immorality flooded me and I felt deeply ashamed. What right did I have to lead him on, to let this friendship move beyond the platonic? I could just have been a decent friend. My sexual dance card was already over-full. What perverse greed was this, what perverse gluttony for more and more men to notch on my bedpost?

I cannot un-see his shocked humiliation when I said no, I can't, and then told him we should no longer see each other. He accepted it, though, civilly enough. It was not the heartbreak of love I cursed him with, but the heartbreak of his lot in life, having been "allowed" to glimpse something more. I cannot un-see this former geek lover, with his open mind, decent command of English, and curiosity that allowed him to see the world beyond his borders.

It is too easy, in this era, to point out that he was not offering me love, just himself as an apprentice to my privileged upbringing so that he could return to his girlfriend with the benefit of his romantic education. It is easy to claim a no-fault separation, and reject the guilty conscience. When I finally left the company, and Hong Kong, he asked if he could have the MOMA-imitation plastic chairs and coffee table in my flat, which I gave him. They were off-white and compact, suited to the tiny spaces of our city. By then he was engaged. It was the closest he could come to slapping me in the face.

Why pin the blame on myself, an immature donkey girl?

But to pretend blamelessness is to live the unexamined life. I was wrong, wrong, wrong. When you hold all the cards you do not, no, *should* not seduce into your game one who is bound to lose. We say, as women, that we need a level playing field. Yet when I could have leveled it, I did not. Morality is more than just for public display. It matters in our private lives, perhaps even more, because no one might ever see or hear or know.

Yet it is that un-removable bee stinger that troubles me most. What I know now but wish I knew then is that for many years after this moment, I would still engage in conflicted affairs of the body and heart. I have never been a fan of *Sex and the City*. It strikes me as hypocritical, a pretense to leveling the playing field when, in fact, the real desire is to perpetuate happily ever after marital bliss. It would be many more years before I could define an honorable way to couple, before I could leave behind the desire to show off my "superior" womanhood. Power corrupts, regardless of gender. Just as shucking off the past and never taking responsibility is the no-fault slippery slope which may, if we are not careful, collapse all semblance of our civilized world. Today, Kristen Roupenian's "Cat Person." What worse dystopia tomorrow?

*

The third time, a female professional acquaintance who wanted to be more of a friend. She could tan dark, like me, and we both readily eschewed the pure ideal of white Chinese skin, content with our natural pigmentation. She was also from Hong Kong and traveled as much as I did, possibly more, even to places that then seemed exotic to us, Bahrain and Dubai. Her career path had been tougher than mine, harder scrabbled, far less privileged. We met sometime during the last few months at my airline job, by which time I had already decided to quit and disappear to Greece to write. Already I was transitioning—the book of the day was Gail Sheehy's *Passages,* which I never read but probably should have—jogging from the straight and narrow to the crooked and jagged path. What I didn't know then but wish now I did was that I would have to tread all four paths, and many, many more, because a single fork in the path was already dead-white imagery.

Her name I have forgotten, but shouldn't have. What I do remember are her wild, curly locks, almost a soft 'fro—I wondered if foreign blood had flowed into the river of her Chinese heritage—and strikingly large eyes. She had a beak-like mouth, thin lips, and small, even, very white teeth. Let me bluntly stereotype: The "average" Hong Kong Chinese man would have given her wide berth, but the "average" white man on our waterfronts would have trailed after her, salivating.

It is possible she and I met on board a flight, but memory is the crookedest path, and most historical facts are irrelevant in the long run. We became acquainted, that is a fact, because we were both in marketing, even though I was trying to remove its malingering hold on me in favor of "art." I had the grandeur of ideals! To write, to live free, to be an unfettered woman, to escape the bourgeoisie of my birth, to abandon the Chinese world of my origins in favor of an international literary self. Marguerite Duras and Doris Lessing wrote my guidebooks, and *The Second Sex* was still not yet past a use-by date. The problem of being twenty-something is that you believe you need never grow old. I had a better handle on mortality at eleven-plus, when I used to imagine the death of my parents, as well as my own eventual demise.

Our acquaintance was short. I remember little of what we did together except for one conversation. Where we were or what surrounded us has vanished into some twilight zone. What remains are her smile, her bared teeth, her dark complexion and beautifully coiffed black hair, her sharp red outfit with its fitting skirt, her high heels, her throaty laugh, her voice lowered as she said *I love to travel and talk to men, especially Western ones, don't you?* And then, without missing a beat, *They're so much better for sex.* It was a perfect T-Zone moment, when the protagonist finally realizes the inescapable horror of her situation. I did not respond, but she kept at me, wanting to share what she likely considered the similar shape of our lives.

In our contemporary shorthand, I "ghosted," "unfriended," "blocked" her. Resisted *this ebony bird beguiling,* afraid to confront the truth of my existence. As this was even before voice mail, I took most of my social calls at work, where a receptionist or secretary took her messages that I never returned. Eventually, her calls stopped. I cannot un-see her absence or my own mean-girl spirit. What's good for the goose only applies to one goose, alone on her hill. *Mommie Dearest* loves you, or at least, until she doesn't, which is when, as the young screen version Christina Crawford says, "she can make you disappear." Had I heeded Poe's raven in this instance, I might have trod an easier path in my endlessly examined life.

*

In later years, well after my terrible twenties during which these three sightings occurred, I would encounter many other naked strangers. I would continue to make the mistake of believing that there, *but for the grace* of some spiritual force, was the face of my own fate. It is only now, in connecting what I *cannot* un-see to what I *should not have* un-seen, that the meaning of this oft-used phrase comes at me in full bloom. It is a pretentiously kind notion, a shudder of existential horror at *this*—a victim of bullying, war, school shooting, bombing, terrorist act; a homeless panhandler; the blind, maimed, deformed, insane, or otherwise "othered" human being; the collaterally damaged. It is easy to shudder at such strangers, followed by looking away. It is only now, in re-looking, re-seeing, even re-hearing, that a re-envisioning occurs. I could have been less neurotic and still lived an examined life. But don't ask now—that's possibly the subject of another essay, to replace what could've and should've with what has been, is, and will always be.

Instead, allow me to re-see in exchange for just a little grace.

Wars

JERALD WALKER

I am about to read at a Veterans' Hospital. My audience will be a dozen men who have experienced combat and, as a result, lead troubled lives. Some of these men are drug addicts. Some are alcoholics. Some abuse their families and others abuse themselves. All of them are required to be in attendance for my visit. Not all of them, the hostess informed me, are pleased about this. One by one they drift into the room, each carrying a pencil and notepad, and if they harbor any bitterness toward me they express it only by sitting as far from me as they can at the seminar table. When the seats are filled, the hostess rises and gives a brief introduction. I take the floor.

It is an intimidating thing to read to a room of men who have fought in wars—men who have experienced brutality and death with an intimacy few others have or ever will. I am relatively at ease, though, because, having been raised on the notorious South Side of Chicago, I have had intimate experiences with death and brutality too, though never for a second do I confuse my wars with theirs. Still, I feel a sort of kinship with this audience as I read stories of my troubled youth, stories that, by the slightest twist of plot—had I accepted my father's pleas to end my delinquency, for instance, and join the military—could have resulted in me sitting where they are, staring stone-faced at a writer as he's risen from his chair with a book in his slightly trembling hands. By the time I'm half-way through, my hands have steadied. And their faces have softened—at least, that is, until I'm done, when the hostess tells everyone to open their notebooks for the writing session of my visit. The prompt: Describe a memorable event from your youth. Would I like to participate, the hostess asks, and I say Sure, why not? She hands me a pencil and a sheet of paper. Because I am here, with these men, I write about Buggy.

It was 1973, the height of summer, and I was trapped on the hood of a car, waiting for a chance to make a break for home, or for my friend to discover that his German shepherd had gotten free. Whenever one of my neighbors came outside, I waved my arms and yelled, "Milo's loose!" and they hurried back inside, all except for Buggy. He casually strolled down his front stairs, sipping from a bottle of Coke.

I was nine and Buggy was just back from war. His mother had been saying Vietnam ruined him, but he looked all right to me, only disoriented and confused sometimes, like there was something he'd forgotten and was struggling to remember. I warned him again. This time he squinted in my direction, as if trying to comprehend, or maybe just trying to see past the glare of the sun boring into my back. I didn't want to be outside anymore. I wanted to be in my air-conditioned house eating my mother's fried chicken. I hoped Milo was hot and hungry too, that at any moment he'd trot off in search of a patch of shade or a bone. But for now he was content to sit right below me, exposing the yellow teeth that, three years earlier, he'd sunk into my cheek.

When my brother and I had entered our friend's back door that day, growls had filled the air, which caused our friend to assure us, as he had for the six months we'd known him, that Milo was harmless. So far that had proven to be true; I guess that was what gave me the courage to try to pet him. A short while later I was on a hospital gurney feeling the tug of nine stitches as they closed my wound and shuddering, as I still shudder nearly a half-century later, from the memory of Milo's lunge.

Buggy took another sip of Coke. Now he was standing in front of the low hedge that lined his parents' lawn, only twenty yards from Milo and me. I glanced around, hoping a squirrel or cat would send Milo off in another direction, away from Buggy, but any chance of that was lost when a belch shot through the silence and reached Milo's ears. Milo snapped his head around. Buggy belched again before lifting the bottle to his lips. Milo darted toward him and stopped midway, as if giving his opponent a fair chance to flee. It wasn't taken.

Milo torpedoed in low and was met with a kick to his face. He backed away, barked, and then dove forward, this time getting hold of Buggy's right leg and trying to rip it off. Buggy almost fell but he gathered himself and started pounding his bottle on Milo's head, Coke spraying everywhere, like celebratory champagne. It took a dozen or more blows until Milo released his grip. He barked some more before slinking toward his home, his long tail wrapped beneath him, pressed against his belly.

The hostess, after ten minutes, tells us to stop. She asks for someone to share what he's written. At first no one volunteers and then hands inch into the air. The first story is about a mother's cancer; the second is of a father's abandonment. And so it goes until we've heard from everyone except for the man who sits directly across from me. His notepad, I see, is empty. The hostess, sitting on my left, can see this too and doesn't press him to participate, saying only, after he declines her invitation to do so, that her memory sometimes fails her as well.

But as he'd held his pencil an inch above his notepad, I saw the expression on his face, and it reminded me of what I cannot forget about Buggy's.

He watched me approach after I jumped from the car. When I reached him he kneeled and pulled up his pant leg; blood covered his shin as it had covered my face. I asked if he was okay. He didn't answer, turning his attention instead to his empty Coke bottle. He frowned and chucked it to the lawn. And then he rose, now looking disoriented and confused— not like a person trying to remember, it occurred to me, but like a person struggling to forget.

X

JOSÉ ORDUÑA

It happened in the basement—that much I remember. I went down the stairs and turned my head just in time to see X handing the small container to the young man. I couldn't really see it clearly, it could have been anything, but I knew it wasn't. I knew what it was, and I knew who the young man was, even though I didn't know his name—I'd never seen him before and I'd never see him again. The young man was in the process of standing up, and X's arm met his at a 45-degree angle in the dim light of one bare lightbulb. A few large men sat at the periphery, their faces illuminated by the light of their phones. My weight on the last stair produced a creak that broke the tableau. X turned to look at me. The young man retracted his arm. And it was over.

*

What I can't remember is if X had shaved his moustache by then. He looked just like his brother Y, so much so that I sometimes confused them. Once, he pretended to be Y for a

33

school meeting for Y's son. The teacher had interacted with Y dozens of times, but she didn't have a clue it was X she talked to that evening. Both had thick, push-broom moustaches, and up until X suddenly shaved his, I thought I'd never see either of them without one. In fact, both of them had, on separate occasions, told me they'd rather die than shave it off. Then one day X's was gone. He never said why, but it was clear that it was to avoid looking like Y, or more precisely, it was an effort to make sure other people could clearly tell them apart. After what happened in the alley during the cookout, everyone was spooked, and then a few other things happened to a few other people and everyone moved a lot differently after that. I think X must have sensed that the world was constricting around him, which it was. I think he wanted to make sure his brother didn't catch something meant for him.

Maybe that's when he started using, or maybe that's when he started using more, or more consistently. In reality, I have no idea how much he'd been using, for how long, or with what sort of frequency. I do know that he seemed a lot jumpier without the moustache, always looking over his shoulder when he walked his dog, peering out the window when he heard a car door slam shut, never leaving the house—even to get the mail—without what he thought could protect him. Which, as it turned out, couldn't.

When I was young, he taught me how to steal. But more than that, he taught me that stealing was what you did if you wanted something you couldn't or didn't want to pay for. It was a small pocketknife I'd wanted that was only a few dollars, which he could have easily bought, but didn't. Instead, he grabbed a box of underwear out of our cart, opened it, and tucked the knife inside. Then he looked at me like, *See?* I remember that it happened in the Cermak Plaza shopping center because the sculpture that used to be there—eight stacked, full-sized cars skewered on a giant spike—will always be tied to the weight of the small red knife hitting the center of my palm as we walked into the parking lot. The exhilaration of doing something that was not only wrong, but illegal, made my heart pound in my ears. A moment after we'd made it out to the parking lot, Z, who was X's cousin but was really like his brother, and who'd seen it all go down, grabbed me by the shoulders, squared me up a couple of inches from his face, and told me to go back inside to put the knife back where I found it. I did, and when I came back outside I saw X and Z screaming and grabbing at each other violently. X stormed off, and no one saw him for a couple of years. When he came back there was something different about him, and everyone could tell.

Years later, when I went looking for the eight stacked cars—a sculpture I never knew was called *Spindle*—it was gone. I read that it was demolished with a crane and that parts of it had been cut to pieces. By that time, the experience of setting out to see a building, sculpture, park, or store that was anchored to a childhood memory only to encounter its absence was becoming disturbingly frequent. The candy store owned by the old Polish lady, the house on the corner where that guy used to yell, Maria's house—all the old houses that looked like regular working people lived in them—disappeared. So many of the places I went looking for were replaced by investment vehicles owned by real-estate investment firms. People's homes—the places where they laid their heads, taught their children to live, conceived those children—were turned into speculations on commodity markets.

*

In the late '90s, right around the time the first multistory condo building went up a few houses down from where my family rented our first apartment, I watched John Singleton's *Boyz n the Hood*. It was the first film I remember seeing that spoke directly to me. I knew a Doughboy, and had seen plenty of Officer Coffeys. We had too many Rickys, and I remember seeing a Brenda chasing one of her kids into the street, swinging a power cord wrapped around her fist and a bulky black ankle monitor strapped to her leg. Among the many experiences I recognized, one scene articulated something I'd started to feel but couldn't fully conceptualize. It's the moment Furious, standing in front of a billboard that reads "CASH FOR YOUR HOME," addresses his son, Tre, and his son's friend, Ricky.

"You listening?" A few neighborhood people—an old man, a few G's drinking 40s, and some kids—walk over to where Furious begins his address. "They bring the property value down. They can buy the land at a lower price. Then they move all the people out, raise the property value, and sell it at a profit." An old man, who'd been listening to Furious's explanation, challenges his assessment in a way I'd heard my grandmother talking about our neighborhood countless times. "Ain't nobody from outside bringing down the property value. It's these folks," he says, pointing at the G's. "Shooting each other and selling that crack rock and shit."

In a medium shot filmed during the last two months of 1990—a year preceded by a series of government reports and investigative exposés that revealed US government involvement in South and Central American drug trafficking to the US—Furious asks the old man how he thinks the crack rock gets into the US. "We don't own any planes. We don't own no ships. We are not the people flying and floating that shit in here." The camera cuts to Tre listening to his father. "I know every time you turn on the TV that's what you see. Black people—selling the rock, pushing the rock, pushing the rock. Yeah, I know." The old man, now off-screen, is audibly agreeing, "Oh yeah. Yeah. Right. Yeah!" Tre watches Furious, but more than that, his eyes cut back and forth registering what's happening among the people in the crowd. He watches his father articulate a street-level political economy that begins to dissolve the antagonism between the old man and the young G's by rallying them around the roots of their common immiserization. "The best way you can destroy a people: you take away their ability to reproduce themselves."

*

X died childless and alone just like countless young people from around the way who fought and died for neighborhood blocks that were later easily appropriated by capital without firing a single bullet. Some of the ones who survived are still locked in cages for entry-level weight while Elliot Abrams holds government office and continues to shape the misery of Latin American populations. As a young man, X left his country, his family, and everything he knew in the middle of an economic crisis known as the "lost decade," a period brought on by unscrupulous lending by US commercial banks; the precipitous raising of US interest rates by chairman of the Federal Reserve Paul Volcker; and the privatization, liberalization, and austerity imposed by the International Monetary Fund and the World Bank. Before I received the news of his death, they'd already removed X's body, and shortly after he was interred, the bank began the process of seizing his house. While she was still mourning, his wife was forced to leave, and I'm not sure what happened to all the things he'd risked so much to acquire. It's been nearly a decade now, and I never remember his death date as it approaches until the early fall of each year, when I start waking up panting because I've dreamt about him. Often, it's about that day in the alley. The different ways it could have played out. If that man had raised his arm and made a different decision. If everyone standing behind X, all the children and women and men who had nothing to do with any of it had caught that man's sorrow. In the chest, or the stomach, or the neck, or square in the forehead. Sometimes they're about seeing his body in that box, packed with Styrofoam for the long journey back to his hometown across a border. I remember feeling grateful that his mother was long dead so she didn't have to see any of it. Often, though, the dreams are about that moment in the basement.

It's like hundreds of slightly different images stacked on one another—it conjures feeling but it's useless as an image except to communicate very rudimentary shapes. I used to think this was something like a worn-out tape, but it's really closer to the opposite, a surfeit of information. Sometimes the memory is triggered by something specific: hearing a pair of owls call to one another across a field, seeing his colors, seeing Y. Other times, it just pops into my mind. When it's like this, out of nowhere, it's startling, like pushing a door at the same moment someone on the other end pulls it. All at once, I'm standing there, staring into his eyes. In one recollection he's got that mustache, and in another he doesn't. One moment I can see that it's a small plastic container with a blue lid that he's handing the young man. In another, it passes between them without me seeing a container at all. If he had the moustache, there might have been time to intervene. Maybe something forceful enough could have knocked him off the course he was on, one most of his people could see was leading to something like a coffin in the underbelly of an international flight. But no one did anything. No one seemed able to move on it. And no one did. If the moustache was gone, it was almost certainly too late. And it's very likely that it was too late either way.

*

On the morning of my twenty-fourth birthday, he came to my place and asked me what I wanted—something he'd never done before. Despite some reluctance, I gave in and we ended up in Barney's, where I'd never bought anything, but where an ex-girlfriend had once gotten me a pair of three-hundred-dollar jeans. I pointed at some sneakers that cost a third of what my parents' monthly rent was, and when the cashier rung us up, X had to ask her to repeat herself when she spoke the price. When he was sure he hadn't misheard, he just chuckled, pulled a fat wad of bills from his pocket, and fingered out several crisp hundreds, barely making a dent in the wad.

X didn't like parting with his cash. His life looked a lot like mine does now, like someone just in the middle class, and he shared the aversion I have to wasting money on things like sneakers. I imagine his came from the experiences he had earning it. Mine comes from guilt. I almost double over when I think about how, as a kid, I used to beg my dad to buy me Air Jordans when he worked as a dishwasher and his shoes had holes in them, or later when, on more than one occasion, I crossed paths with him at one, two, or three in the morning as I came home from drinking his money away at a bar and he left to go work in a windowless freezer room the size of a football field for a wage that was never there at the end of the month. For some reason, I didn't feel anything like that about getting those shoes that day. I wore them until they came apart years after X died, and then threw them away.

Recently, I came across the extra pair of laces that came with the shoes and I was compelled to keep them. I found them as I was packing up to move from Albuquerque to Las Vegas—another move farther west from Chicago, where my parents live and where X died. I packed them in a small box I marked "very important," and when everything settled after the move, they somehow ended up dangling from the eye socket of a calavera that's become the centerpiece of an ofrenda I never meant to make. I bought the skull in Tucson after I'd volunteered with a group that hikes into the

Sonoran Desert to leave water for migrants being murdered with thirst. Beside the skull there's a necklace that X used to wear, and inside the cranial cavity, there's a toothpick I found in the breast pocket of a forty-year-old shirt that belonged to my great uncle Romeo—the man who raised my father—of whom I have no memory, and whose funeral my father wasn't able to attend because he couldn't leave the country knowing he might not be able to come back.

I spend long stretches staring into the eye sockets of the skull because it's in my office, where I read and write for hours at a time. Often, I don't register what I'm looking at, but sometimes I do, and when that happens, I think of several things: how, as I'm staring into the blackness of its eyes, there's someone out there, walking, being killed or skeletonized in the desert because of more than a century of this country's brutal hemispheric policies; how, even if you do manage to cross that line, it follows you, sticks to you and marks you, often for life; and how X, who was undocumented, would today be left out of most immigrant advocacy because the realities of his life would put him at odds with the squeaky-clean image the mainstream of the immigrant rights movement mobilizes around.

Other times, my focus goes to the red laces in particular, and I think about those shoes, and thinking about them bothers me now. It bothers me that it didn't bother me then, even though I knew what it took to get that money. I'd seen the half-moon scars on faces, the paranoia, the young men with canes, the entry and exit wounds, the archipelagos of keloids on the scalp. People call it *easy money*, but there's nothing easy about it. Rentiers' money is easy money, at least for them. X's money was a lot of things, but easily acquired was not one of them. Maybe I made him drop that kind of cash on sneakers to punish him because I knew and was angry that he would die, angry because I believed *he* knew he would die, and angry that we both knew he wouldn't or couldn't do anything about it.

Whatever the reason was, I remember receiving the news and feeling like someone had just recited something I'd written down and read to myself countless times already. I remember thinking in words, *It happened,* and among the blunt heartache I felt a sliver of relief because the anticipation of it was over. Some of the people who knew him talk about his life and death like some cautionary morality tale, but what I saw was something else. What was available to him when he arrived was the life available to most undocumented immigrants—decades of back-breaking, low-wage work that grows in precarity and compresses in value as your body breaks down with age—a life like my father's, who today works at a grocery store making a wage that's barely enough to keep the lights on and won't be enough when he faces his middle age's first serious illness. I think a lot about what kind of choices I would've made if I'd have been faced with those possibilities, and the only thing I've come to feel with any degree of certainty is that morality would have little to do with it.

Today, when I go back to Chicago to visit my parents, I often drive through the old neighborhood, where they no longer live. They were pushed farther west, where the rent is still something they can pay, and where I worry about my mom's bus ride and walk home from work, and my dad's walk from the car to the front door. Their neighbors are other Latin Americans who haven't managed to fully escape what they fled. I don't go to X's neighborhood, or drive by the house where he lived, because I don't want to see it. I'd like to be free of that memory, or more precisely, I wish X had been able to live and die in a way that would allow his memory to rest.

Love and Death in Mexico

KRISTEN IVERSEN

The first and only bullfight I ever saw was on the last day of the year. I was deeply in love with a man I had met two years earlier, a tall, gentle, ardent man who was open to things like love and adventure and, as it turned out, bullfights. On the spur of the moment, in a rush of starry-eyed enthusiasm, we decided to go to Mexico to celebrate New Year's Eve. I had been to San Miguel de Allende previously and was captivated by this town of artists and ex-pats, wealthy families from Mexico City and locals who shared their language and culture with more tolerance than we Americans probably deserve. Called the heart of Mexico, San Miguel is the birthplace of the Mexican Revolution, and the city has a heartbeat as strong and vibrant as the bulls we saw in the arena that day.

We jumped on a flight the day before New Year's and then found we couldn't get a hotel room. Founded by the Spanish in 1511, the city is a maze of steep cobblestone streets and historic Spanish architecture, old-world shops selling dried flowers and pottery alongside a few new-world eyesores like Starbucks and Burger King. The streets were crowded that day. Indigenous *Otomis* and *Nahuas* kneeled on blankets and sold fruit and peeled *nopales* as tourists—Canadian, American, German, French—toted bags bearing designer brand names, clothing and perfume that could be bought at the expensive shops. A New Year's Eve concert was scheduled for el Jardin, the beautiful garden square, and the town felt electric with excitement. Every hotel and bed-and-breakfast was booked. Finally we found a room above a small shop selling hearth-baked pizzas, Casa Chiquita. The streets of San Miguel are lined with hundreds of tall colonial doors, many distinctly carved, behind which are hidden shops and elegant courtyards. Each door was different and yet they all looked the same, and we walked past a door twice before realizing it was what we were looking for. We entered and we were immediately struck by the delicious smell of homemade pizzas in the open-hearth oven, flames licking the bricks. A man whose face glistened with the warmth of the room greeted us in Spanish and asked us to spell our names in a small spiral notebook he pulled out from under the wood counter. He then took us up a short flight of stairs at the back of the shop and showed us our room, one of four rooms the owner rented to tourists. Our room was small, the bed nearly filling the entire space, but there was a tiny bathroom with a view of the cathedral, the Parroquia de San Miguel Arcángel. Outside, a few more steps led to a rooftop terrace where we could be served beers and pizza the following day if we wished.

That first night we fell into bed exhausted, dusty and sweaty from the flight, the bumpy drive through the dry hills from the Leon airport, and the long walk tugging our luggage over the cobblestones. We made love quietly, furtively, afraid we might be heard through the paper-thin walls, giddy in our successful escape.

✳

I had heard of the bullfights in San Miguel. My first visit to San Miguel, years ago, had been post-divorce and my feelings were still raw, my freedom unsteady. I was there to teach a writing workshop just as my own confidence as a writer had been severely shaken. Everything about San Miguel—the dry fragrant breeze, the flowers, the sunsets—felt beautiful and alive with possibility. I had stayed in a small family-owned hotel with some of the other teachers, and one night the outspoken leader of our tremulous group suggested it might be a good idea to go up on the hotel roof with a bottle of tequila. If we lay flat along the edge and craned our necks over the parapet, he said, we would be able to see into the edge of the old bullring, where a bullfight was taking place that very afternoon. To make the story even better, he added that the bullfighter would be female.

The thought of witnessing a bullfight made me feel slightly nauseous—did they actually kill the bull, I asked? Was it even legal? No one knew. And I had never seen or even heard of a woman bullfighter. I crawled up on the roof, buoyed by a second tequila shot. I could see almost nothing through the narrow gap between the buildings except a slim edge of white wall, the blur of a crowd, and the brief swirl of a red cape.

Later that night, after a dinner of *suiza* enchiladas near el Jardin, I walked back to the hotel with a group of students, young women in their early twenties. The street was dark and the girls' loud chatter bounced off the Spanish walls, their shoes clattering on the cobblestones as they walked behind me. The street felt closed-in, the doors and courtyards shut for the night, but then we passed a street-level window, singularly flung open to catch the cool breeze. I glanced in. Even now the image is seared in my mind: a tousled white sheet draped over a man's feet, his back arched up like a cat, face plunged between the raised thighs of a bare-chested woman. Her back was pressed against the headboard and her long dark hair streamed across the pillow. She must have heard our approach for she looked over just as I passed. Our eyes met.

I called to the girls, urging them to hurry. I hoped they hadn't seen it. I felt alarmed, embarrassed. My cheeks burned and my heart beat a little faster.

The woman was pleased I had seen her.

*

The next morning George and I rose and went in search of breakfast: eggs with green chile and strong coffee. We had slept soundly and we were starved. In San Miguel the yolks of eggs were a rich deep butterscotch, a result, we were told, of the chickens eating buttercups and other bright-colored flowers that grew so abundantly in the town. They were the most surreal and best-tasting eggs I've ever had. Hearts and bellies full, we strolled back toward el Jardin and that's where we saw the poster: *San Miguel de Allende Corrida Fin De Ano 2016*. A dash of red and black depicted a bullfighter swirling a cape in front of the horns of a bull. We pieced together the few Spanish words we understood to try to decipher the details. End-of-the-year bullfight. Six bulls, three bullfighters, 4:30 p.m. that very afternoon at Plaza Del Toros, the bullring I had glimpsed in my first visit to San Miguel.

"Should we go?" I asked George.

"Of course," he said. We shared a similar approach to travel: open eyes, open mind, open heart. We wanted to see everything. A Spanish-speaking friend had helped us make dinner reservations for that evening at a rooftop restaurant, where we could watch the fireworks over the square. "How long does a bullfight last?" I wondered. "I have no idea," George replied. We decided it was definitely worth risking dinner. At four o'clock our worries about finding the bullring disappeared— we simply followed the crowd. A series of turns down the cobblestone streets led to a narrow alley, where people pressed in as close as if they were trying to get into a New York subway. George paid for two tickets at a booth staffed by a cheerful young woman. Vendors sold trinkets and leather wineskins. By the time we reached the entrance I was sweating from the sun and the press of bodies. We climbed a short set of steps and walked around the edge of the ring until we found two seats in the sun three rows above the floor of the ring, coincidentally just below the stand of the president, the judge of the event. The stands were already nearly full and the crowd was mixed; men in groups and couples and a few children. We sat beside two older men in broad white hats who already had purchased beers and cigars from a vendor walking along the row, and a younger man to my left, extremely well dressed, who made me feel self-conscious in my sunglasses and jeans. George, with his dark hair and mustache, blended in more or less except for his height. I seemed to be the only blond in the stands. No one seemed to care. We felt excited, soon to witness something exotic, forbidden, historical, perhaps disturbing.

"Beer?" George asked.

"Sure."

"Cigar?" he joked.

"No thanks."

A man approached us selling cardboard trays of snacks, glossy red nuggets that everyone seemed to love. Were they nuts or some kind of bug? We couldn't tell. "No gracias," George said, and we both felt a little embarrassed.

The band began to play, a raucous quartet of horns and drums. My stomach felt a little queasy. I wasn't sure what to expect, really. Would I be horrified or fascinated? I loved animals almost to a fault. I'd always had pets, dogs and cats and horses. Years ago, when I raised white doves in cages, a newborn baby dove caught its claw climbing out of the nest and broke its leg. The veterinarian built a miniature cast, and then a miniature Styrofoam throne to keep the fluttering, bug-eyed creature as stable as possible. Of course, it was impossible— the leg never healed, and after weeks of effort we had to snuff out that tiny breath with a dab of chloroform on a cotton ball. And then I had a $500 vet bill and couldn't pay rent.

I cried, and it wasn't for my pocketbook.

Bullfighting is a blood sport. George and I knew this. Marriage can be a blood sport, too, and we knew that as well. We'd each endured bitter divorces, with a few other failed relationships along the way, and we each had been on our own for a while. You don't near your sixth decade of life without having been to more than one rodeo, so to speak.

I close my eyes during horror movies. I can't watch movie chase scenes that end in gunfights. I've experienced the death of loved ones but I've never actually watched a person or an animal die.

I was determined not to look away.

Ernest Hemingway, who counted many bullfighters among his friends, wrote, "Bullfighting is the only art in which the artist is in danger of death."

Many countries have outlawed bullfights, or limited them to some degree, but in San Miguel the full tradition endures with a long history behind it. Spanish-style bullfighting is called *corrida de toros* (the running or coursing of the bulls) or *la fiesta* (the festival). Three bullfighters fought on this sunny New Year's Eve: a *rejoneador,* who fought the bull on horseback, and two matadors who fought on their feet. It would be *Mano et mano,* according to the poster: one by one, the bullfighters facing six bulls from *La Macarena,* each bull weighing somewhere between one thousand and thirteen hundred pounds. Of the three men, *Rejoneador potosino* Rodrigo Santos was the most experienced. The son of ranchers who had wanted him to become an agronomist, he'd spent nearly thirty years on horseback in the ring. Twenty-three-year-old José Garrido was a relatively new matador from Olivenza, a small town on the Spain–Portugal border. Garrido had three years of experience and already had a small following. The new kid on the block—the hometown favorite—was twenty-two-year-old Fermín Espinosa Díaz de León from Aguascalientes, Mexico, known as Armillita IV. Armillita came from a family of bullfighters and was expected to carry on the family tradition. He was a baby when he attended his first bullfight, and as he grew he'd been schooled by his grandfather and father. "My father has been my mirror and I see myself reflected in it," he told a reporter.

In addition to the three bullfighters and their attendants, there would also be a contest for the hometown crowd, where local men would physically wrestle a bull to submission and prove their promise as potential matadors.

When I was a small child, my Grandma Claire read me *The Story of Ferdinand,* the tale of a young bull who preferred to smell flowers rather than fight in bullrings. During the summers I spent at my grandparents' house, Claire's fingers stroked my forehead as I sat in her generous lap each night and we read *The Story of Ferdinand* over and over. Ferdinand was a gentle soul, refusing to cavort with the other young bulls on the ranch. It wasn't until he accidentally sat on a bumblebee and leapt in astonishment that he was sent off to the bullring. At his debut, he ignored the matador and instead was entranced by the ladies sitting ringside, beautiful flowers in their hair. He plunked down in the middle of the ring to sit and fully enjoy the view. The matador broke into tears, and Ferdinand was returned to his peaceful pasture.

Published in 1936 by an American author, *The Story of Ferdinand* has been a perennial bestseller: It sold more copies than *Gone With the Wind* and has never been out of print. Nonetheless it drew controversy. Some saw the story as a political allegory promoting pacifism, particularly as it came out just after the outbreak of the Spanish Civil War. Gandhi admired it; a critic in Cleveland claimed the book would corrupt children. Hitler ordered the book burned as "degenerate democratic propaganda." The *New York Times* maintained the book was about nothing more than being true to oneself. Tens of thousands of copies were provided free to Germany's children after World War II to encourage peace.

In 1951, Ernest Hemingway wrote "The Faithful Bull," a short story that begins with the line: "One time there was a bull and his name was not Ferdinand and he cared nothing for flowers."

It's not uncommon to see wedding parties in the streets of San Miguel, sometimes several times a day. The bride in her flowing white dress walking beside her groom is followed by a parade of family and friends accompanied by tall dancing *mojigangas,* puppets on stilts, fifteen feet high. Often there is a mariachi band. The puppets are traditional, dating back to the 1600s when the Spaniards brought over their antecedents, *Los Gigantes.* Originally created to honor as well as poke fun at administrators and local politicians, these days more often than not the puppets portray a goofy, kitschy bride and groom. A wedding is sacred and also a circus. The locals know this. Parody and irony prevail.

It's in the streets of San Miguel where the old and the new exist peacefully, at least for the most part. The cobblestone alleyways are crowded with pedestrians, cars, small ATVs, and donkeys—often carrying saddlebags of flowers—but there's not a single stoplight in town. The flow of human and animal traffic is constant and seamless.

San Miguel has a dark and seamy underside, too. During my first visit to San Miguel, as writers we were obligated to visit the infamous bar La Cucaracha. Dating back to 1947, La Cucaracha over the years had been home to more than a few literary talents, particularly the beatniks, and Neal Cassady had lay down and died on the railroad tracks just a few blocks away after reportedly drinking himself into oblivion. The four of us had to have a look. An innocuous exterior led to a large, darkened room with pictures of skulls and nude women on the walls. A large plastic cockroach hung on one wall. We pushed up to the bar to order shots of tequila, and I looked up and noticed the TV behind the bar was showing soft porn interspersed with Bugs Bunny cartoons. There were very few women in the place, and the men looked, shall we say, a little rough around the edges. We put coins in the old jukebox and danced on the sticky floor. I was ready to leave then, and the others wanted to stay. One of the male teachers walked me out to the curb and gestured for a cab. "I want to make sure you get home safe," he said gallantly as he opened the taxi door. We rocked at high speed—high speed for cobblestone streets, that is—until we reached the solid gate of my *apartamento*. As I reached in my bag to pay the fare, the driver—a man around thirty or so—abruptly leaned back and kissed me on the lips.

I was stunned, completely caught off guard. I jumped from the cab, leaving the money on the seat, and ran to the door.

He dutifully shone the headlights on the gate until I opened the lock, and then sped away.

Was I angry or flattered? Did he think I was some kind of lady of the evening? Does this sort of thing happen to any woman who goes to La Cucaracha?

I didn't know what to think.

Bullfights in San Miguel follow the classic three stages or *tercios,* lasting about twenty minutes each, in which lances of increasingly shorter length are driven into the bull's back just behind the head. The final plunge is intended to be fatal. If a bull performs extremely well and shows exceptional bravery, it will be spared, but this is extremely rare. Everything depends on the skill and nerve of the bullfighter and the strength and tenacity of the bull. A brave matador will bring the bull's horns very close to his body. It is said the matador who risks nothing will never be great.

Our bullfight, like all bullfights, began with the *paseíllo,* the ceremonial entrance of the bullfighters and their entourage. Led by the *rejoneador* astride a magnificent bay-colored horse, they entered from the opposite side of the arena, circling around to the president's box just behind us, where they paused and gave a salute. Another *rejoneador,* the less famous one, no doubt, followed on a palomino the color of tawny gold with creamy mane and tail. Two horses came next, wearing heavy orange, quilt-like armor on either side of their saddles. These horses, we would learn, were buffers for the bull's rage when the *rejoneador* made his strike. It wasn't until 1928 that horses were protected and expected to survive the bullfight; traditionally they wore no protection and the bull would often injure or even disembowel the horse. Still, it's not unusual for them to get bruised or injured. After the horses came the matadors themselves, José Garrido and Armillita IV, in brilliant costumes. They looked very young, slim and fit. If they were nervous we couldn't tell; their faces were set and expressionless. A team of two horses pulling a dray brought up the rear. They would drag the bull's body from the arena after each fight, after which time the bull would be butchered and the meat sold at market or served in local restaurants.

The parade exited and *Rejoneador potosino* Rodrigo Santos reentered the ring. The crowd roared. Clearly, he was as famous as a movie star, and he had the looks to prove it. Santos wore a formal-looking black jacket with a gold waist, black chaps, and a wide black hat with a slim green ribbon. His horse was a beautiful, heavily muscled Andalusian horse, a traditional Spanish breed, with a silky brown coat and a dark, braided mane and tail. The mane was braided with black and green ribbon to match the rider's hat.

Santos took the horse through his paces. I knew enough about dressage to recognize some of the steps: the piaffe, the half-pass, the bow down on one knee. The horse moved in a graceful, exaggerated movement, dancing on its hooves, closely controlled by the rider. Santos then dipped his head to the president, uttered a prayer to the Virgin of Guadalupe, and the bull entered the ring.

In a recent interview, Armillita IV talked about being the son and grandson of bullfighters and how important it was to carry on the family tradition. He had to work hard to stay fit—bulls can move very quickly—and he runs every day to stay in shape. He loved the moment when he dresses for the bullfight. A matador is distinguished from his assistants by his *traje de luces,* the satin suit of light which is decorated in gold or silver. The hat of a matador is flat-topped, with a round knob above each ear representing the bull's horns, although not all matadors wear hats. The moment he is fully dressed, Armillita IV said, is "when everything changes."

*

Bullfighting has a long tradition in San Miguel de Allende, going all the way back to the Mexican hero Ingacio Allende, a captain in the Spanish army who came to support the movement for Mexican independence in the early 1800s. Allende himself was a *rejoneador,* a bullfighter on horseback, and the town was named in his honor.

The tradition has changed over the years. Juan Belmonte Garcia, known as Juan Belmonte, was a famous bullfighter born in Seville in 1892 and went down in history for his technique of standing erect and nearly motionless, allowing the bull to come within inches of his body. The technique was born of necessity—Belmonte's legs had been slightly deformed since childhood and yet he was determined to become a bullfighter. Previous bullfighters danced and jumped around the bull; Garcia planted his feet firmly and made the bull move around him. Bullfighting was changed forever.

Traditional bullfighting is still legal in Mexico, and the largest bullfighting ring in the world, holding sixty thousand spectators, is in Mexico City. But overall, bullfights have been on the decline. In San Miguel small protests have been held in the public squares, with lectures and poetry readings on animal rights. The international Humane Society strongly condemns bullfighting. Some who support bullfighting like to point out that the bull lives three times as long as other cattle used for meat, and its comparatively comfortable life is led in meadows and forests rather than cattle pens. In 2014, professional bullfighters in Bogota held a strike of their own, a hunger strike against a ban passed by the city council. "Stop us killing bulls and we'll kill ourselves," they chanted.

✳

"Suppose a painter's canvasses disappeared with him and a writer's books were automatically destroyed at his death and only existed in the memory of those who had read them. That is what happens in bullfighting." —Ernest Hemingway

✳

George and I occasionally talked about death, not in a morbid way, but in the practical manner of those who had reached a certain age and had come close to it once or twice. I felt my closest brush with death was literally the sense of breath on my neck. I was jogging in the foothills of San Jose, California, along a steep trail not far from my home. There had been rumors of a mountain lion coming down and snacking on cats and such, but I didn't take it seriously. I loved that trail: the trees, the brush along the side of the trail, the birds, the breathtaking view of the city. I had left my earphones behind as the spring air seemed filled with birds and I didn't want to miss their voices. Suddenly I sensed something, a heavy movement in the brush just behind me on the right. I heard a low growl, an ominous snarl, and I felt the breath of an animal. It was very close.

I thought immediately of something I had heard in summer camp or Girl Scouts or maybe a show on TV: Raise your arms to make yourself look bigger, and start shouting. I raised my arms. I shouted. And I turned to see a flash of tawny, muscled flank spring down into the brush and disappear.

I ran the rest of that mile waving both arms in the air, shouting and singing, scared out of my wits.

George's experience was much more intense. In his early fifties he'd been diagnosed with neck cancer and his chances were slim. Doctors told him that in order to save his life they would have to cut out his tongue. He refused and found a doctor with a different opinion. He endured months of treatment—surgery, chemo, and radiation—and then the tumor returned. There was a moment when, faced with what seemed inevitable, he felt complete emotional surrender to his fate. Calm, ready, and slightly pissed off. "I remember thinking gee, I thought I had more time," he said.

There's never enough time. This is what scares me. There's never enough time.

✳

Just before the first matador, José Garrido, entered the ring, I stepped over George's legs and walked up the steps to join the line at the women's restroom. A line of men sat with their beers along the top bar of the arena, shouting "Olé!" and "Bravo!" A woman stood at the *baño* door, collecting pesos and handing out tissues and feminine products as needed. She smiled at me. A younger version of her was selling snacks and soda pop. No one took notice of me. I bought two more beers and returned just as Garrido entered the ring. He wore a sparkling blue *traje de luces*. To my inexperienced eyes, he seemed competent, completing the series of stylized passes with the cape, the bull playing along with interest if not an obvious degree of fury. When the first lance drew blood, I was shocked but not sickened. The more dramatic moment was when the dray team came in to drag away the bull's body, suddenly lifeless and heavy. Garrido's third bull was spectacular, snorting and charging and ferociously digging his front hooves into the sandy earth. Garrido responded with grace and style. With each successful swirl of the cape the crowd sang "Olé!" After ten minutes or so, Garrido turned his back to the bull, faced the president, and raised his hand. The crowd responded by waving white handkerchiefs. After a tense moment, during which I was certain the bull would take his chance to finish things off, the bull was given an *indulto.* He seemed to understand this, and galloped exuberantly around the ring, head held high, and vanished out the gate. George and I imagined him being transported to green pastures where an adoring harem awaited him.

The famous bullfighter Juan Belmonte became a close friend of Ernest Hemingway, who attended countless bullfights and greatly admired the sport and the art. In 1961, at age sixty-one, Hemingway was faced with numerous health issues and an apparent inability to write. He committed suicide by gunshot. Belmonte, also beset with health issues and no longer able to ride a horse, committed suicide by gunshot in 1962, one year after the death of his friend.

It's common for bullfights to offer events and competitions for new and aspiring bullfighters called *novillitilla.* This is where most young bullfighters first earn recognition. Many towns also feature events for local young men—or women, I suppose—to try their hand at the sport. In groups of six, they stand at the edge of the ring and are then allowed to "play" with a young bull. There are no lances; the bravados are expected, in single file or as a group, to wrestle the bull into submission. Most of them end up on their backs. On this day there were two such events. At the first, following the *rejoneador,* a line of six men stood ready to go. They looked like a local moving crew or perhaps a squad of Santa's helpers, and there appeared to have been some heavy drinking going on. Responding to a signal by the young man at the front, they tackled the bull head on, one after the other, aiming for the comparatively safe spot between the bull's back between the wide horns. The bull happily and seemingly effortlessly tossed each man into the air. He seemed to relish the experience. No one seemed significantly hurt.

The second group, following José Garrido, was not so lucky. The timing was off, the aim was bad, and the bull was mad. Bodies flew in every direction, and one man was gored. The bull gave him a final stomp with his feet. His body was completely still. A group of people with a stretcher hurried out—there is always a doctor, a surgeon, and an ambulance standing by—and they quickly carried him out of the arena and behind the wall.

We never learned if he survived.

In *Death in the Afternoon,* one of Ernest Hemingway's best-known works, mid-paragraph—and apropos of nothing—he incongruously takes a swipe at Virginia Woolf, whom he taunts for being so bold as to think that women are as smart as—or smarter than—men. I'll pause here to take a swipe at Ernest Hemingway, who's not the only one who can write about bullfights.

In the final stage of the bullfight, the *tercio de muerte,* "the third of death," the matador enters the ring alone with a smaller red muleta and a sword. A good kill is when the sword goes in quickly and efficiently to the hilt, cutting the heart or aorta, and the bull dies quickly, sinking to his knees in a prayer-like position before falling, flanks and then shoulder, to the earth. A bad kill not only causes the bull to suffer needlessly, but it draws shouts and boos from the crowd.

By the time young Armillita IV entered the ring for his final encounter, the sun was dipping behind the horizon and long shadows fell across the far side of the ring. Confidently he strode out into the ring in a *traje de luces* of green and gold, richly embroidered, with bright pink socks. I thought of my own sons, who were nearly the same age as this boy pretending to be a man. Armillita's body was slim, his back arched, and he faced the bull squarely, the muleta in his left hand and the sword in his right. Their eyes connected. With his head the bull followed the movement of the cloth as Armillita swung it in a full pass, and then he charged. The horns came within a hair's breadth of Armillita's arched body.

"Olé!" sang the crowd. And then another pass. "Olé!" The man in front of us shouted "Bravo!" Armillita turned his back to the bull and tipped his chin to the sky in a gesture of acknowledgment or artistic arrogance, I wasn't sure. His expressionless face had taken on a new look. He stood in perfect composition, like a ballet dancer at the end of a spectacular pirouette. *I can come this close to death,* he seemed to be saying, *and make it look effortless.*

But then the spell was broken. In his next pass, Armillita dropped his cape. The bull nosed it in disdain. Armillita retrieved it and struggled to recover his composure, but the bull had grown testy and wiser. In the next pass, Armillita stood slightly off center and the horn of the bull caught him in the leg.

"Oh!" I exclaimed. George gripped my knee. The crowd grew silent.

Armillita walked to the edge of the ring. Was the doctor standing by? Armillita ignored him. We couldn't tell how badly he was bleeding. The satin of his right thigh was stained a dark red.

But then he turned and walked calmly, methodically, to the center of the ring. If he was in pain, he didn't show it. Again

Armillita unfurled the muleta, casting it wide and then whip-
ping it again and again. The bull swung and swirled around
him, a whirlwind of motion within a hairbreadth of his hips.
In our third-row seats, we could hear the hot angry snort of
the bull and the boyish call of the matador: "Hey! Hey!"

Then, like a child before an altar, Armillita dropped to his
knees. He faced the bull directly, straight-on, with only ten
feet between them. He dropped his arms to his sides and let
go of the cape and the sword. Holding the gaze of the bull, he
inched forward on his knees. The intimacy between bull and
man, so close before, was now almost unbearable to watch.
Armillita folded his arms over this chest, cocoon-like, and then
in a single motion he ripped open his shirt and jacket, exposing his naked chest to the bull. Both were bleeding and panting. For a long moment they held each other's eyes. Slowly
Armillita rose to his feet and picked up his sword and muleta,
turned his back to the bull, and walked away.

The bull held his charge. The crowd roared.

Armillita glanced briefly at the president's stand, then
turned back to his bull. The animal was heaving. Exhaustion
shook his frame; the blood from the *banderillos* that pierced
his flank had dried. Then the bull seemed to pull himself
together. Armillita raised his cape. The bull lowered his head,
shook his shoulders, and charged. When the sword entered
the bull's body it went to the hilt, at the right spot, and the
bull sank to his knees almost instantly.

As George and I walked back through the bullring alley to
the exit, we stopped by one of the vendors. She sold balloons,
candy suckers, and plastic-topped wineskins adorned with
cheesy scenes from the bullfight. The more attractive items
were tiny Christmas ornaments, *traje de luces,* daintily adorned

with tiny stitches and sequins, a perfect replica. We bought one. We waved to the man at the gate, who told us in Spanish that he hoped we'd had a good time. Silently we walked back to our room above the pizza parlor, where we washed off the dust from the bullring and changed our clothes. We made it in time for our dinner reservation, a narrow, rooftop restaurant up a long flight of stairs, high above the city, and from there we toasted the city with margaritas made with fresh lime and very good tequila. Over dinner we watched fireworks over the square and indeed across the entire cityscape—everyone seemed to be celebrating—and on our way home we lingered at el Jardín, where a live band rocked a crowd that filled every corner of the plaza. The bells of Parroquia de San Miguel Arcángel announced the strike of midnight.

Later that night, on the cusp of 2017, we made love above the pizza parlor. I don't know if anyone heard us. I didn't care.

Late in the summer of 2016, *rejoneador potosino* Rodrigo Santos officially announced his retirement. "I have lived intensely a great passion," he said, "and I feel very lucky, because not many people have the luck to live a great passion." He then added, "And I am very hurt." Over the course of his thirty-year career, Santos had survived six gorings and twenty-seven fractures. José Garrido was now a full-fledged matador. Fermín Espinosa, Armillita IV, continues in the tradition of his teacher and grandfather. He has a strong following on Twitter.

Two years and twenty days later, on a winter day filled with sunshine, George and I were married in his hometown of New Orleans. In our vows, we each expressed gratitude for the opportunity to be loved by the other, how we loved our companionship and the creative spark we shared. George noted that we had fallen in love with an almost reckless abandon. I emphasized George's gentleness and sense of adventure. From the very beginning, nearly five years ago, we had felt we belonged together. We celebrated with a party on a riverboat that chugged steadily up the Mississippi River, oblivious to the January wind.

The officiant, a man with a kind face and long gray hair pulled back in a ponytail, had spoken of how marriage is a resonance of love, born of individuality and union, which brings both incredible strength and fragility. He quoted Ram Dass, "We are all just souls walking each other home."

As our families and friends danced in the ship's ballroom with their colorful masks and Mardi Gras beads, I thought again of San Miguel de Allende, that city of beauty and blood, and young Armillita, his chest bared, fully entrusted to whatever fate might bring.

Lizard Brains

NICOLE WALKER

In chapter 1 of Robert Sapolsky's *Behave,* a book about the brain, he implores the reader to read the appendix if the reader is not a neurologist. Although I am a doctor, I am not that kind of doctor, so I read the appendix, even though it was another seventy-five pages to read of an already long book. In the appendix, Sapolsky explains how the neurons, chemicals, and synapses in the brain send and receive stimuli. If you read the appendix suspiciously, you might see the way Sapolsky argues for a particular understanding of how life impacts brain. It doesn't matter how much your brain explodes with vigorous chemical, synaptic, and dendrite signals. If there aren't enough receptors to receive those signals, your brain's really just wasting energy. It is through time, and experience, that the brain can be stimulated to grow more receptors so those stimuli have some place to go. So, if you really want to encourage your brain to do certain things, amp up the stimulation, and eventually, the receptors will be there to receive. You can grow your brain. It's like learning. Can you unlearn?

The amygdala is the oldest part of the brain. It's the part that fights or flees or freezes. When my husband and I went to one of our two total counseling sessions with Stan—our psychologist and the guy that played in a band my husband had been invited to join—he showed us a baby's toy he kept in his office. The toy, many-colored plastic rods, connected together. Compressed, the rods turtle up, fold into a tiny ball.

"This is your brain during an argument," Stan said. "Everything is all tight and clenched." You can't think about anything except the small insults your husband barks about "Who put this away dirty," and the extra-clever retort of the wife, "At least I put things away." Back and forth, the insults go inside the ball, sending more anger-making signals. The anger bounces off the walls of the small ball. The lizard brain, the oldest brain, cannot escape the immediate danger of losing an argument over dishes.

"But watch this." Stan takes the baby toy and pulls the rods. The tiny ball opens into a gigantic sphere, a web of connection, a plastic color wheel, a moon of possibility. "This is open-mindedness. This is prefrontal cortex. You could live in this space, it's so wide. All you have to do to get there is breathe." Just looking at the sphere as it expands in the office calms. I could stay with Stan forever.

I blame my brain for most things. It's so good at making receptors for traumatic memories. Childhood should be filled with happy memories. And mine is. But there are these other memories that pull like gravity.

Age 4. Baby sisters, twins, in the backseat. I'm in the front. My mom pulls down the garage door by its rope handle. Her thumb. The garage door folds flat. My mom manages to raise the door again to release her thumb.

Age 8. A thud. Vibrations through the ground. My sisters' bedroom window. From there I can see my dad lying prostrate. He doesn't move. The ladder still stands against the roof's fascia. The bottoms of my feet absorb the sound.

Age 10. Male babysitter. Tank top. Who wears a tank top at age ten? Who thinks a ten-year-old's tank top is sexy? Who removes that tank top when he's supposed to be making ice-cream cones for the ten-year-old and her seven-year-old sisters?

Age 10.5. Chad with the cystic fibrosis. Chad's perennial cough. His funeral.

Age 11. Fifth grade. Stain on the back of my jeans. Stain on the chair of Ms. Townsend's math class. I cannot stay seated in place forever.

Age 12. Looking out the window of my sister's room. A different house from the one where my dad fell off the roof. The boy I like hasn't called. He drives by. He doesn't even slow down.

Age 13. My mom says to my dad, "You have mustard on your lip." He may as well had the blood of virgins on his lip, the way she said it. It was the first time she found out about Julie.

Neurologists say the prefrontal cortex doesn't fully develop until your late twenties, but that the amygdala is able to pock its lizardy surface with pits from the get-go. My fear is this: A pock-marked brain looks for new memories to fill the caverns of trauma. Can you make a trauma out of a non-trauma if your brain is filled with holes?

Age 26. He stands on a bridge in Dublin. He's mad or I'm mad. Something something about Guinness.

Age 28. Why does he have to wear that shirt? It has holes in it. My mom is going to be there. Please change your shirt? Please.

Age 32. Barry Weller tells me my scansion of George Herbert during my final exams left something to be desired. Too-tall boots. Snow. Miles of walking in the dark and cold in strict iambic pentameter. Some amount of pyrrhic falling down.

Age 35. Why did he burn the steaks? Why?

Age 41. Barbs were exchanged. Names were called. No clue what the argument was about but it's a long walk in the cold at night uphill and downhill until I'm too tired to be mad anymore about what?

Age 43. Walking. Why is there so much walking alone in the middle of the cold night? Something something something, didn't do the dishes? Are household chores worth this many steps?

Some people are better at breathing than others. Some of our brains lock down in tiny-sphere baby ball mode. Sometimes, there's a million tiny receptors in your brain waiting for the signal punch. Like a hole yearning to be filled, the receptors, multiplied, might go looking for some stimulus. Perhaps those receptors, trenched at an early age, habitually look for certain stimuli. Perhaps memories tumble into those receptors and get locked there. My question for my brain—can you, brain, build some receptors that lock down the good memories as hard and tight as you do the bad ones?

There are good memories in there, too (just to emphasize the theme of the anthology, which is what we wish we hadn't seen?): swinging on swings and riding on bikes. Climbing fences. Scurrying down hillsides toward the creek. Crossing the creek rock by rock. Salamanders in the window well. Holding the two-by-four while Dad hammered. Peeling potatoes for Mom to slice. Mom singing in the car. In the hallway. Down the stairs. He top-of-the-head kissing. He in the rain, dancing. Portland walking and Iceland hot-potting. Apple crushing and Fremont wading. Ocean body surfing and ocean diving. Searching for oysters. It has all been mostly good, dear brain. Dear happiness receptors, listen to your mother: Dig some new divots. Hoe some more rows. We've got memories of this faithful life to store.

To Love Me,
Or the Intruder's Tattoo

MARY CAPPELLO

I wished I had never seen his tattoos. I wasn't supposed to see them, and especially not in this way. Seeing them could be a sign of his having done something shameful, or could have been a sign of his being shamed; yes, he had done something shameful, and now he was being more-than-shamed in turn, transformed via snapshot into a nonperson, the inscription of a personal poetry reduced to signposts on an inspector's grid. It wasn't that they sought to know him by displaying the tats; it's that they sought to know the *who* of his crime—to flesh out the criminal's visage, to align the marks with a composite stereotype. "They" may have been police; they may have been forensic pathologists; they may have been newspapermen. They no doubt had tattoos of their own, significant and private as dreams, such secret singular signature knowledge, emblazoned upon an inner eye. We can be sure they weren't readers, but crude interpreters along the order of butchers who cleave meat away from bone and sinew, which they then slap, weigh, wrap, and charge.

If I say that I will never forget what they did to him—
the horror and obscenity of their violation—I am probably
only telling a half-truth, because in the years since the tattoos
appeared in the newspaper, I have neither pressed to resolve
the facts in his case, nor have I found a way to preserve the
beauty of who he was, enduringly. Is that too strong an either/
or? As though reparation was up to me, as though restoration
were possible? And who am *I*, anyway?

The photos were of a dead body not a living one, and since
the news article was digital, they were there for everyone in the
world to see. They pictured the body of a person I had loved
with the sort of love for which there is no word—the form of
caring regard that teachers come to have for their students.
To watch someone bud and blossom as I did Jesse is a rare
and beautiful thing; and then to feel the kindling of warmth,
beyond warmth, kinship. Many a day, it helped Jesse to know
in talks we'd have in my office that we had a share in something, the something of class beginnings, the onus of being
first-generation college students from the working class: "Jesse,
do you know where I come from?" I'd say, and now I'm here,
and you are here, and you will go even further still.

It was in the dark zone of a late January in New England, just a few days before the start of a new semester, when
another student called to tell me that something terrible had
happened—that Jesse had died, that the circumstances of his
death were mysteriously violent, that it might be possible to
search for the facts online, but that nothing as of yet was clear.

With a few spare clues, I searched and found the first article that had appeared: the attorney general's office of a town
two states away was "seeking the public's help" in identifying
a man in his twenties or thirties who had broken into a house
in the middle of the night, where he held an elderly man hostage for several hours. The intruder died by a gunshot wound
to his head, but police could not yet tell if he had shot himself,

been shot by the elderly man, or a combination of the two: It seemed he may have required the man to pull the trigger of a gun he pointed toward himself. Since the intruder was without ID—he was missing his wallet—the authorities decided to display photographs of his tattoos with the thought that someone would recognize them, and thus the gruesome anonymity of what I would never be able to un-see. I felt the shock of his body-in-parts in my stomach before I began to cry. There was the pornographic quality of their being without a face, less dignified even than medical specimens; there was the fact of how a person—your body—could become public property overnight. The alleged "search for identity" was and was not sincere since the article already took great liberties in identifying the man. The original report is no longer searchable, but I remember wild conclusions—he was a punk, a liberal, a communist, a hippie (the language was ahistorical and retrograde), possibly a prison escapee, a drug addict, a hobo, a pariah, a fiend.

Another article described the marks—there were four in all—with the cold calculation of their respective locales:

on his left forearm, a typewriter;
on the inside of his left wrist, the words "be here";
the word "ques" on the back of his right arm, above his
    elbow;
and the words, "to love me" on the inside of his right
    wrist.

Taken alone, and out of this context, the tattoos create a poignant poem. In their recast ghoulish guise, the photograph of a typewriter tattoo pierced and haunted me most. For one thing the scale of it in the original article made me think it was splayed across his stomach rather than traced inside his forearm. There was a close-up of his hair oddly magnified with a grouping of freckles intertwined. The hair at first seemed like pubic hair, and one of the keys, his navel. Of course Jesse would have a typewriter tattooed to his arm—he was a writer. And then I recalled my own professional "card" at the time before digitized identities had yet set in, and my personal logo of choice: a similar sort of old fashioned typewriter. Was it possible we were joined at the wrist in ways I'd never imagined? Closer than close can be? At the very least, if not in cahoots with one another, in the classically Freudian sense, "identified" with one another? On closer look, I surmised that his typewriter, though it was old enough to have a bell and return arm, was more like a prototype of an early electric model whereas mine was clearly a manual.

I felt sick at the thought that I should not be seeing this—it was not my right. That, in fact, no matter how well and in what particular way I knew him as my student, I had never seen Jesse's tattoos. I couldn't get past the intimacy of his hair, and it seeming so alive, on a forearm I was expected to understand as dead. I couldn't bear the thought of the hands of a stranger turning his body over to angle his arm, then offering it up for a snapshot. Inspecting the tattoos more closely, I saw marks that made even less sense. The typewriter was inked in black and white and lightly smudged as though rendered in charcoal; his freckles with clear edges appeared as dots of mauve-ish-brown; but there were indeterminate blots of red among the keys. No one had bothered to wash off the stain of his blood.

If I say I was "no stranger to violence," what could that possibly mean? And what might you picture if I told you that I "grew up in a violent neighborhood"? For me, there are no pictures, just sounds—and that's half the problem with such tutelage. In place of lessons in sewing or baking or the proper way to tuck the corners of the sheets, I was trained to grow accustomed to violence whose consequence was to plague me with sounds stripped of their visual counterparts, noises that intruded into consciousness with no apparent cause—a repertoire of thwacks, snaps (of rubber gloves), cracks (of skulls), or the *thwuonck* that a large van door makes as it closes across a cavernous darkness; a voice, reedy; a voice, choked; a tat tat tat of gunfire; the soundless sound of a body draped and limp. At the center of such memories, two words that remain essential that I can't explain: *fumble,* and *snap.* I've dropped something or am myself dropped, I'm groping; something snaps into place while something else breaks off, beyond repair. Writing takes me back to the fumble, and the pretense of assured grace.

I taught Jesse during a period in my life when I brought "portable pleasures" to my office to deal with overwhelming ambient anxiety. Back then, it was as though a thousand concerts were going on in my brain at once, with the occasional crash of tympanum causing a sudden spasm in my fingertips or an uncontrollable fluttering in my heart. "Competing desires" is how I always thought of it, but none of my intellectualizing ever stopped me from breaking out into a sweat. Where other people stowed bourbon, I kept a cassette player with Schubert and Bach.

I first met Jesse in an introductory class that no one else wanted to teach that semester and that the chair had assigned me as punishment for disagreeing with her on the subject of a recent hire. It was a course with a deceptively simple-sounding title; it was nothing more and nothing less than "The Poem." If you start with the question "Which poem is *the* poem?" you have enough material for a lifetime. The first impression Jesse made was that of a wise-cracking clownishly cool dude who strutted into the room and who thought it'd be okay to answer my earnest questions with jokes. I can't recall what exactly I said, what sort of look I may have given him, how the weather shifted to move him from jibe-maker to acolyte, but overnight he came at the material with a kind of utter reverence, and he was especially excited the more we began to explore the relationship between poetic practice and ideology, invisible presences, or in Chomsky-speak, "the unspoken framework for thinkable thought."

He wore oversized flannel shirts and sloppy light-colored jeans layered also with a sweater, a film of previously smoked cigarettes, thickly framed black glasses, a mop of curly brown hair, and on top of that a hoodie that he seemed to hide inside to keep a bad case of still-lingering teenage acne from view. He didn't so much talk as rap, and bore proud traces of being a white man from a mostly black neighborhood; he was also one of the few white students in a program hosted at the university that seeks out disadvantaged kids who might otherwise not ever have access to a college education. The program is called "Talent Development."

In time, Jesse took three classes with me, each one more advanced than the last, culminating with a class in literature and medicine focused that semester on a subject that now seems either terribly apropos or terribly ironic. Using books like Elaine Scarry's *The Body in Pain* and Susan Sontag's *Regarding the Pain of Others* as our guideposts, we studied the limits and possibilities of language to represent psychic, bodily, or social pain. If the inevitability of suffering is what joined us humans at the hip, so must the imperative that we love one another. The emphasis was on an ethics of care as the thing that connected us fundamentally as humans.

You have to imagine Jesse fired up about a new idea, jotting notes quicker than his mind could put them down, notebooks and journals filled with his thoughts in dark pencil. Jesse enjoyed accompanying his raggedy ensemble of ill-afforded clothes with at least one detail that bespoke "businessman," so you have to imagine him pulling his shaggy notebook out of an overly shiny boardroom-ready briefcase that he carried around, all the while keeping a straight face. Usually in our meetings, he'd bring some recent reading or recent thought about how to combine his knowledge of political science (his major) with poetry (his passion) to address inequality in the world, but you also have to imagine him occasionally telling me he wanted to flee. He was nearly finished, in his junior year, but he didn't know what to do with an unbearable feeling: "I just want to check out," he told me, in my portable pleasure borne office, "forget college, drive, disappear." And I'd respond with counsel, and I'd call this distress, and then we'd critique the privatizing of depression—it's not your fault, it's as much cultural as personal, I'd try to explain, and I'd call the counseling center for him while he was still with me in the room, and he'd pull himself up and take himself there, he'd help himself to work with those unbearable desires to exit.

On another day we're discussing the poem by Auden about Icarus's fall from the sky, how suffering happens when someone else is eating or just walking dully along, and the snow is falling faster than the patter or the passion of our talk. At first we don't notice it; then a wild wind howls and shakes the window; then we pause together and watch and wonder, maybe we'd better go, but I say, "Well, it's not going to get better and it's not going to get worse, let's keep going! You were saying?"

And he goes on, "Look, Prof Capp, this is what I want to know: Are the 'masters' Auden talks about imperialists and is that why this dude thinks poetry makes nothing happen? Did this guy read Brecht?" He reads aloud again the opening lines of Auden's "Musée des Beaux Arts": "About suffering, they were never wrong / The old Masters: how well they understood / Its human position: how it takes place / While someone else is eating or opening a window or just walking dully along."

And then he puts a poem in front of me, not Brecht's, but one of Jesse's own, it's an aphorism that goes, "The phrase no pain no gain was written by an Imperialist." And then he pulls some Brecht from his briefcase, "Did Auden read Brecht, because Brecht said it better," and he gives me three disarmingly direct lines, none of which can anticipate the one that came before it, each one deepening the devastation, and the conditions that dictate how or what we see, look at, or watch. The first line is seemingly benign: "I beheld many friends, and the friend I loved most . . ." But this is followed by the image of a swamp that the poet walks past daily into which his friends have sunk.

Jesse thinks Brecht can be harder to understand—there's a lot of irony that passes for logic that is difficult to parse; Auden seems easy—all that lyricism—and he's suspicious of the lull. So Auden emulated Brecht and made something worse, he concludes. Can I emulate Brecht and make something just as good? Jesse asks, and gives me:

I do not like what
    I see

So my body becomes
    Numb.

Numb like my mind
    Aspiring to be
        poetic.

*

In the aftermath of the release of Jesse's identity, there was a riot of details that needed sorting in order to determine "what happened." His friends were caught up in this as much as the press, but we kept returning to a cardinal violation: that reporters and police who had the power to represent him, bent on composing a story, did not know him and could not see him for who he was. And yet I wonder in what sense as his teacher I claimed to know or to *see* him? If there's one thing I need to set straight, it's that I'm not interested in being real in my classroom; nor do I want to know who my students *really* are. The classroom is an island of difference—why, otherwise, would I have chosen to spend so much of my life residing there? It doesn't pander to a common denominator; it's not Dunkin' Donuts. Like a novel, it's a fantasy space, rife, not exactly with ego, but with imago, or ego *ideals*. Like a novelist inside her novel, or a poet inside his poem, a student inside a classroom gets to practice being someone else who is and is not yet them; the classroom is a place where I expect my students to find something better than the self they know themselves to be, whether or not they choose to display that figuration publicly to me or their fellow classmates.

There are things that my students will never see about me, that they cannot see if learning is to take place, like my hideously misshapen feet and embarrassing habits of mind the details of which would only prove irrelevant, distracting, and unhelpful to the larger enterprise. This isn't to say I only put my best foot forward in the classroom or present myself as a perfect specimen of humanity. Usually what I perform is a hyperintelligent clown—I know what I don't know and I lay the ground with questions intent on glorifying pratfalls, slips, and descents into the abyss. It's not me in there—it's a projection, a tryout, an essay.

Sometimes my students keep secrets that I wish they hadn't, and that makes me wonder if the ground we lay together obscures what's really important in spite of my best efforts at fostering surprise. I remember the time, in a separate room than the one I knew her in, that I heard the contralto voice of a student fill up every molecule in the room, leave her body, take us out of our own, and return again to the quiet of her unassuming comportment. I remember thinking: How could I not have known she had this in her? What else was I missing about my students' boundless capacities or cultivated talents?

One of the first thoughts I had when I learned of Jesse's violent, untimely passing wasn't to picture his literal brain exploding into bits but all of his learning fled out a window. I remember thinking that if he was dead, all of the lessons I had taught him were dead and gone as well. Where did that thinking go? I remember feeling that there was not a lesson available that could help him, and that all such thoughts made his death about *me* rather than him.

There is so much about him I never knew, will never know, and cannot see—like the depth and nature of his sorrow, or what broke in him on the day of the break-in, and how it must have felt irreparable even as it moved like an arrow to a target that said, "This way out." There's a school of thought that says we are responsible for our students' failures, but what about our students' crimes? Against themselves or others? Was this anything like the way that parents felt whose children went terribly awry? If a parent's sole purpose and role is to keep their child alive from the get-go, what do you do with a child who refuses? I'm thinking of a friend whose eleven-year-old daughter became increasingly anorexic, and the force of her command, thou shalt not, thou wilt not take charge of *my* life, of *my* death. I'll never forget the harrowing minutes, days, and hours in which she performed the ultimate refusal: I imagined her saying, "I refuse to be *your* daughter. I'm only daughter to myself."

On the night of Jesse's crime, on the night of Jesse's death, it snowed. I know this because police reports included this detail as evidence of his movements. In my grief, I sometimes comfort myself by picturing the shape of Jesse's footprints in the snow en route to a random stranger's house. I try to picture their shape before they disappeared and imagine someone vital there. Everyone has a need to tell the story a particular way—even to think of it as a story in the first place, whereas, for me, Jesse's life and death can only be sensed, not plotted, possibly woven, through a glass darkly. And I know that even those traces of a vibration of a memory of his life in me risk being made over again into a justification of the principles that govern my own sense of self. The pieces might be fractured, but they will no doubt tend toward keeping my worldview in place.

So it was with journalists whose accounts I felt compelled to read as I sought to know what in god's name had *happened*. The attorney general's office had asked for the help of "the public," but god keep us from *their* hands, because when I read the "public's" comments, I felt stabbed and gutted as though it was I who had committed the crime. If the journalists fed us half-baked tidbits of morbid curiosity, the town's criers used language as a blunt instrument, a cudgel, or a sort of short, squat caveman's bat. They patted themselves on the back for their foreknowledge of inevitable invasion by a faceless enemy and the need to fortify their arsenal. "Do yourself, your family and your neighbors a favor and buy a firearm and learn how to use it," they shrieked. They referred to Jesse as a "perp," "a punk kid," a "scumbag" who was "rightfully dead." They referred to their neighbor as a "gentleman from a multi-generational family" and wrote the word "LONG" in all caps to emphasize his long-standing dyed-in-the-wool relationship to the town. They misheard the facts in the case, confidently asserting that the eighty-two-year-old man defended himself with a weapon, which they then used to rationalize the purchase of guns: "Perp tried to strangle him and Mr. Smith was able to retrieve his firearm and put a round into the bad guys [sic] head. This guy will NEVER rob, steal, cheat, rape, murder or hurt anybody again." A person who was more circumspect about what had actually happened, suggesting that "the perp may have shot himself dead," suggested without the least bit of irony, "I'm not one to spread rumers [sic] so I won't comment again until I hear the facts in the morning at the coffee shop." Others, like the audience at a lynching, dealt a deftly sinister blow, lurching toward metaphor: "Another self defense success story, glad to hear things turned out well and one less waste of oxygen is on the streets."

One full year after Jesse's death, the attorney general's office posted a "final report" regarding what they came to call the "home invasion/suicide." It is dotted with unprocessed conclusions and with details whose relevance is vague at best. It reports the "body of a white male found lying on a kitchen floor"; the observation that the "individual was wearing layers of clothing, suggesting that he may have been homeless"; it references "fresh footprints in the snow leading from the park-and-ride to Mr. Smith's residence." With "no criminal history" and no "illicit substances or other drugs in Cook's system," it finds no way to "explain" Cook's "erratic behavior." It hints at impersonation, or a suspicion around Jesse's show name: "Jesse Cook also went by the name of Ques Paulson. It has been determined that he performed in at least one Providence nightclub, playing guitar and singing under the name of Ques Paulson. A YouTube video of Mr. Cook performing under the name of Ques Paulson was also located."

Other details are ones I've tried for many years to turn away from, they are so lurid, so strange, so indicative of a private pantomime Jesse was carrying out, at once entirely his own and like a poor imitation of a B-grade movie. Evidently, Jesse kicked in the bottom panel of the stranger's cellar door, entered through the bulkhead with a gun, asked the man where he kept his money, and disabled all of the telephones in the house. He accused the man he terrorized of having committed crimes and referred to people in photographs in his home as his own relatives. From time to time, he took items from inside the house and moved them to the garage. He poured box-wine onto the floors of the house "as if he thought the wine was gasoline." At one point, he ordered the man onto a bedroom floor, "placed a plywood board and box spring" on top of him and sat on top of it.

These madhouse antics culminate with a "scene" that I can barely bring myself to transcribe. According to the "final report,"

> In the early morning hours Cook brought a gun into the kitchen, told Mr. Smith to stand up, and placed the gun at Mr. Smith's temple. When Mr. Smith told Cook that he would spend the remainder of his life in prison for killing him, Cook then stated, "why don't I just kill myself then?" Cook then took Mr. Smith's hand, and placed it on the gun with his own hand, pointed the gun at his own head, and the gun discharged.

Tacked on to this harrowing scenario is another inexplicable remainder: "Forensic examination of the weapon failed to reveal any identifiable fingerprint impressions."

Jesse Cook was one of the sweetest souls to grace my life, but it still astonishes me how, for so many years, I was unable to hold that thought and simultaneously think about or consider the unsuspecting person whom he victimized. I can't imagine enduring what this eighty-two-year-old man had, and surviving to tell the tale, but when the news first broke, I wove my own version of events in which Jesse was the victim, and the people with money and clout, his tormentors. To this day, a part of me continues to believe that something major here fails to square.

✳

I last encountered Jesse by chance. It was just a few months before his death, on a perfect Autumn Day, Columbus Day to be exact, when I ran into him—I was walking—in Providence. We each caught sight of the other simultaneously across a whirr of cars, and next thing you know we were locked in our usual wide-ranging and passionate conversation. I hadn't seen him in a while, and it had been six years now since he graduated. I told him about the surreal spectacle of the Shriners in their little cars in the nearby Columbus Day parade, and we talked, joyously, we talked and talked till one hour spilled into two and we talked about what we always talked about: politics, poetry, and the daily, the quotidian questions of how to live from day to day. He told me he was just now reading Hawthorne, and Baldwin; I'm sure I quoted Hawthorne on how his real education began *after* his formal training—that's when he really started to read, after he graduated from college, and he read everything then, especially the Puritans; and of Baldwin, how one must read all of him, not just the essays that had been canonized, one must muster the discipline to read the entire oeuvre page by page by page, sentence by sentence, unadorned truth by unadorned truth.

In and out of and between the lines of our talk, Jesse began to express some unnamed trouble. At first, it was just a generalized uneasiness about where he'd thought he'd be by now with his writing, with his music. He asked me about my own writing group and if he could join it. I hesitated. He hinted with greater uneasiness of a mix of trouble—some trouble he was in, some trouble he had caused, with an ever-familiar soul-searching look on his face, the look laced with desire to make it better, to improve, to change something in himself, to change the world. By the end of the conversation, though I asked with genuine concern about what was bothering him, what he might have done, he told me nothing, nothing except to leave me with an impression that he was hard up for money and he had done something to earn it of which he was ashamed. "You know where I am," I'd said to Jesse when we parted that day, "you know where to find me. Just pick up the phone."

I don't know why, but my imagination that day went to prostitution: I imagined that Jesse was prostituting himself and this was what he was ashamed to share. I then renarrated the "suicide" as a tryst with a man seeking sex, gone wrong. The revelation of sex with men would ruin such a man's reputation, so the man killed Jesse. In cold blood. Or, I imagined the presumed victim as the head of the male prostitution ring against whom Jesse was now seeking revenge. He went to the man's house to torment and then kill him, but was killed himself instead, by someone who entered the scene. With no prints on the pistol, how will we ever know who killed Jesse Cook? And who would care? Jesse's own father had suicided; his mother died of a drug overdose. This is what I remembered Jesse to have told me. He was raised by a grandfather who had recently died, and was survived by an aunt and a few apparently distant cousins.

I never reached out to the authorities. I knew on some level that my surmise was absurdist—and it's a good thing, because I later learned that Jesse arrived at the man's house in a car he had stolen in Rhode Island from a woman he had earlier held at gunpoint. To disguise the car, he stole a license plate off of a separate vehicle in the state where part two of his crime spree occurred and covered the original one over with it. So says the final report. When I tried to find an official record of that hijacking online, I came up empty.

Why was he traveling without his wallet? Who had he become? What kind of meaning can be made when truths that we refuse to admit—in my case, that Jesse was capable of holding other human beings hostage with a firearm—crash up against the subterfuge and disconnect, the hopefulness and drive of our imaginations? The trajectory of Jesse's final journey is one in which randomness and premeditation entirely intermix. My most generous reading of Jesse's crimes casts him in the light of a person who himself had been neglected and abused. The man he held at gunpoint was, one minute, his father, and the next minute, his grandfather (recall that he thought he was in his familial home). To get there, he had to go to some place cut off from himself, to some very dark place. Or, let's imagine that he thought he was going home, but when he got there, he remembered that home was a hellhole and a shitshow and he would not be able to find a way out. Jesse died looking into the face of an elderly stranger; Jesse died looking into the face of a terrified man.

Oddly, there's no name for the crime that Jesse may have committed. Do we call this assisted suicide? Coeval-cide? Mano a mano cide? Confrar-icide? I just can't get past the cruelty of his requiring a stranger to play a part in his violent leave-taking. As if to say, "You did it to me! I am not doing this to myself! And you will pay. You will live with it." Or maybe it was just an attempt to feel, at the last, the warmth of another, hand upon hand, before absolute darkness and cold. It was to beg someone to worse than punish him—to erase him, violently, in one stroke; it was to require someone to submit to his will, in return for which, he ceased to be, proving his own will-less-ness. It was to deny what would be left in the wake of his act: the overpowering smell of blood and gunpowder. The sound itself at such close range, enough to burst an eardrum.

It's no wonder that when I reached out to the dean about how we might memorialize this URI alum, I never heard back from her. From the college's perspective, there was nothing here to celebrate, let alone draw attention to. But that didn't stop Jesse's peers from orchestrating a memorial the likes of which I've never seen in someone's honor. Now you have to imagine forsythia—and nothing but—as the delicate bright centering point for a group of people gathered in the round and layered, filigreed, person to person, our heads like bright bobs on stems of mourning, coming together many months after the snow into a blue-colored lounge just a few doors down from my office. It was a program without ceremony built of touchpoints and relays from one person to another telling stories, performing his music, listening to recordings in total silence through tears. How well they knew him, how well they remembered him, how well they cared. They talked about a man I did not know who was a natural born dancer; a basketball player; an artist whom they wished to emulate who did not "use his art to rise." In their eyes, he was legendary, heroic, courageous. When they joked about his food choices, I sensed a class distinction they failed to get—he liked to eat Wonder Bread, Hamburger Helper, and cheese puffs, they laughed. They recalled his stealing trays from the cafeteria to use as makeshift sleds in moonlight; an obsession with dumpster diving; and the time at a birthday party not his own where he insisted everyone get naked and smear themselves with birthday cake.

Everything was there, especially love, but also hints of disturbance, that, in their telling, only made the students uncomfortably laugh. They called him "unique," "real," and a "true, pure artist." One friend described his love of cuddling; another gave us each a copy of a silkscreen she had made in his memory: It was a beautiful portrait of Jesse in profile, looking up, in place of his name, the phrase "gentle soul." In closing, they explained he was a collector—of typewriters. And then they sang a song he wrote made of gorgeously soft notes and hushed lyrics; it was, I'd say, a kind of protest lullaby, with a refrain that could be its title: "In the hour of the folk song, song."

None of us can know how truly loved we are; even if he could have witnessed his own memorial, he could not know. He would find a way to un-see, or to deny that he was worthy. I was thinking this when the young man who had led the event approached me with something in his hand. It was a banged-up, slightly dented blue cardboard folder that looked like it might have spent too much time knocking around in Jesse's faux briefcase, or perhaps it had been dug out from inside a couch cushion covered with cat hair and snack-food grease. The man was gentle in his delivery of what he called a "gift" that his group of friends thought that I should have. They had found it among the few personal effects left in Jesse's apartment. They didn't know what to do with it, or who should get it.

They gave me his diploma.

Am I a weirdo or just a drama queen if Lady Macbeth's "out, out damned spot" begins to ring in my ears during the writing of this essay? What type of essay can arise from helplessness? "*All* essays," another student of mine would say, because the essay is the form most willing to admit of impossibility and of failure.

Unlike an essay, a diploma can neither be given back nor given forward. It has a very limited use value tacked onto the skin of an office wall; it's right up there with lapel pins and gavels, engraved or unengraved, as heavy as they are hollow, inside a room that calls itself a "den" or a display case. And yet in this case it was the bearer of so much genuine meaning, of an honor that could not have been imagined, once bestowed;

of something once met now unmet, fulfilled, unfulfilled, its recipient unable to survive its execution. Had I been its sender, it was now marked boldly with the word *Returned*. But there's more: It came to me at a time when diplomas seemed to be sticking to me like flypaper. I didn't ask for them—or did I? Coming from the working class, I can never, it seems, stop collecting yet another seal of authentication or approval. I hadn't asked for them, or had I? They came to me in droves that year from medical societies where I'd given talks based on a book I had recently written, and awards committees who seemed in competition with one another to be the first to claim the honor of having chosen me for recognition. Diplomas beget diplomas as in the Old Testament, and are themselves testamentary. They're accompanied by clammy handshakes from men who still wear Brill Cream, and signatories, faux satins and laminates, plastic rivets shaped like anemones, bound by rites and rights, they are more *writ* than written, often embossed, certainly gilded. In my study, they are stacked liked ungainly canvasses, propped on a floor, obscuring books on a lower level of bookshelf, suitable for tripping over, ready for the dumpster when my end of time arrives. *All the perfumes of Arabia* can't erase the accumulation of diplomas, and the terrible gift of Jesse's now slivered in amongst them like a curse.

A better artist than myself would have known what to "do" with the diploma, where to place it, how to enable it to shine, to collate, or collage, re-signify. A different artist could have made the thing I had claimed to have wanted to make in the aftermath of seeing Jesse's tattoos in the newspaper, for hadn't I given myself a simple directive thus? *Take up a piece of soft charcoal; recreate his face; compose an essay in soft pencil.* You will laugh if I say that my first approach was to think I could write this essay "off the top of my head," to write in some way that I *never* write—"exactly as I remembered it." You will laugh because you know better than I; trauma makes us stupid.

Recomposition is anything but simple; if it had been impossible to *un-see* the tattoos, the minute I gave myself the task of writing them, I began to see them *everywhere*. At the hairdresser, I set a knapsack I randomly chose from the closet that day onto the floor next to me, and it stares back with a loudly colored brand name, the word *TATTOO*. In the library, there's nobody around, just me and the books, when I'm met by a poster of an old-fashioned typewriter and the words, "the original wireless device." In the midst of this writing, I agree to go to a "holiday bash" even though I worry that I'm carrying this dark material around with me and won't be able to feign good cheer. I'm really playing at being "up" with a drink in one hand and a cookie in another, when a black-and-white image of an Olympian manual hits me in the face. It is literally the only image hanging on a wide white wall of my host's living room, a place I've never been till now. She was giving me a tour when the playful image, even a kind of happy one, appeared, but I experienced it as heavy with an uncanniness that I could not express and certainly would not share for fear of being thought crazy.

There are words for this: *narcissistic projection verging on paranoia*; *unhappy accident*; *meaningless coincidence*. This type-writer belongs to my colleagues; it isn't mine, it isn't Jesse's. It turns out it is Paul Auster's—it's a reproduction that my colleague's husband was gifted back in 2004, he explains ("the year on Jesse's diploma!," I think, but do not say), and it's from a book that Auster made with an illustrator named Sam Messer in homage to his writing machine. Try as I might to drive a distance between this typewriter and the one I was studying just hours before—*It doesn't mean anything! It's just a typewriter!*—I find more affiliations when I read about *The Story of My Typewriter* on Amazon: The book tells the story of "Auster's typewriter and [painter] Sam Messer's welcome, though somewhat unsettling, intervention into that story"; it's a book punctuated by Messer's "obsessive drawings of author and machine." *Taunt* isn't so far from *haunt,* and I begin to imagine that in writing I've disturbed Jesse's ghost. On bad days, I'm convinced that Jesse wants something from me that I cannot give; on good days, I imagine him writing the essay with me—but even then, there's a sense that there is something he wishes to say that I cannot hear, a sign that I cannot interpret, a mark or impression or tattoo that I'm blind to.

More reminiscence than coincidence, I begin to feel stalked by a thirty-page lecture I had once written entirely out in longhand that culminated with the place, and resonance, the punning and the menace of the word *tattoo* in Edgar Allan Poe's "The Tell-Tale Heart." I was recovering from chemotherapy at the time, and had never considered writing out a lecture before, nor was I ever afterwards able to recognize the clear-minded fluent reader who composed the thing. She moved with command in and around the contours of the tale, like a master composer who could name all of its chord progressions, divine its linguistic etiologies, and literally feel the throb in Poe's brain that produced it, the blood that coursed through the veins of an utterly perfect story in which every syllable was and was not a clue to an endlessly alluring unsolvable puzzle. "Meantime the hellish tattoo of the heart increased," Poe had written of a madman tormentor and the old man who was his prey. And I had written: "The word 'tattoo,' which appears exactly adjacent to the words 'tattletale,' 'tattle,' and 'tattler' in the dictionary, derives from a phrase in Middle English, 'Doe het tap toe' or 'Do the tap to,' that is, shut it up; it's a signal for closing public houses. The word later came to refer to a signal for soldiers or sailors to return to quarters for the night given by a prolonged continuous drum beating or bugle call. Generally speaking, a 'tattoo' is a 'continuous drumming,' but, importantly, a drumming that one must answer to, that draws one back, and back again into the fold of one's soldiering. As with so many of the 'signals' in this tale, though, Poe mines this word, too, for both its aural and visual significance—since barely a sentence passes, when the narrator asks: 'do you mark me well?' A tattoo is a sound, a drumming; a tattoo is a mark, a visual sign. But to 'mark,' also means here 'do you hear me?' Or, 'hear me well' deaf reader. If we really want to take this word to town, we could inquire into the relation between 'mark' as hear and 'remark' as utterance (which I can't do just now because I'm in a cabin in the woods without a dictionary). All that I can do for now is notice the telling confusion embedded in this particular word at this particular juncture in the tale: to mark me is to render me subservient, readable, different; to mark me is to hear me, in fact with a degree of attention."

Is it possible we can teach—or soothe or heal—ourselves by rereading work that we ourselves have written? Do our earliest essays contain the seeds for understanding later irresolvables? Or is it simply the case that the essay that I'm currently trying to compose is one that I had written once before but better, with this the weaker, thinner, less luminous version? The failed double, the pale reflection, like the recurrence of tattoo after tattoo, the perfect metonym? Metonyms, otherwise known as substitutes, allow me to look at Jesse's tattoos while looking away from them; they make the unbearable fact of them familiar while keeping them strange, and they burrow down, with each fresh instance, vertically, they replicate and stack, statically, unlike metaphor that moves across, nudgingly and lovingly, exciting inexact resemblances from filial pods. All these metonyms appear for lack of faith in "it" having ever really happened in the first place—in this, they are like diplomas, authenticators; through them, the fact of Jesse's death might show itself, manifest, even, in real time, *occur*, at the same time that they keep him from me, even insulate or shield me from him, like layers of clothing against the cold.

The most striking instance of these ghostly replacements involved yet another book, another story. I'm alone in my study uneasily inhabiting the nebulous between-time of a semester break, too tired to begin the writing that I claim to want to do, and nothing else, but determined to clear a path to my desk, ritually to clear a ground. Mounds of piles of stray papers need to be sorted and placed out of view if only to reveal the thinly yellowing horizon line of my desk lamp, like a flame that needs more oxygen if it's to glow. I'm in the section of my attic study where my literature and medicine books are stacked when my removal of several paperbacks to make room for a fat file causes a hardback book to topple and fly open to a particular page at my feet. It's not a book I remember even owning, and it's probably not a book I'll ever read but one I chose on one of those occasions when a press offered to pay me in books rather than in dollars for a service I had rendered them. I admit to being occasionally drawn to books that promise to tell me everything I would ever need or want to know on a particular subject, and this was one of those. *The Body in History: Europe from the Palaeolithic to the Future* by John Robb and Oliver J. T. Harris sprung open to page 85, upon which appeared two photographs of tattoos displayed much like those that shone in newspaper reports of Jesse's murder/suicide.

I pulled the book into the light to reveal faint black marks on mummy skin, waxen and brittle; a body part that resembles an ankle but that really is a right knee; an area of nondescript plane, a back. The tattoos, comprised of a cuneiform shape in one case, and nothing but short vertical lines in rows of three in the other, belong to what the authors describe as "the most famous prehistoric European body," that of Ötzi or the Ice Man, a fellow who hails from the third century BC, on the threshold of the Neolithic and Copper Ages. The tattoos are the earliest known to mankind.

Ötzi's entirely preserved body was only fairly recently discovered by hikers in a remote mountain pass in the Italian Alps. Various aspects of Ötzi's body led the authors confidently to conclude that he "lived and died in a drama of Copper Age masculinity" (and I think, did "masculinity" really exist back then?), but his remains include one detail "that does not fit," and that detail is the fact of his tattoos. Unlike contemporary attorney generals' offices or newspaper men, these writers take seriously the significance of bodily marks that are meant to be seen and bodily marks that are meant to remain private; of bodily marks that prefigure a community-based choreography of signs, and bodily marks stowed quietly inside the confines of a relationship of self to self. Deducing that these were not meant for public display—they are in areas of the body usually covered—Robb and Harris at the same time refute a popular conclusion that reads them as signs of a highly advanced medical treatment akin to acupuncture: According to this theory, the tattoos, because they are not display-worthy, must have served a purpose, and, based on their location near bones and muscles that seemed to have undergone some wear and tear, they must be signs of a therapeutic method, part of a complex system of care. Though Robb and Harris don't venture much of an alternative conclusion, they nevertheless treat the fact of the Ice Man's body with reverence, describing his tattoos as "the most eloquent witness of the relationality of his body."

While "investigators" were never able to discern in the case of my beloved student even if the gun by which he died really did belong to him, or who pulled the trigger, the number of things researchers have been able to discover about the Ice Man via study of his body is staggeringly precise. By scrupulous examination, scientists have been able to conclude that Ötzi was a lactose-intolerant high-altitude shepherd and occasional copper smelter who traveled far distances to trade in metals. Traces of pollen, dust grains, and tooth enamel tell them that he spent his childhood in one part of the Alps and his adulthood in valleys fifty miles further north. Examination of his hair yields knowledge of what his diet was from several months before: "Pollen in the first meal showed that it had been consumed in a mid-altitude conifer forest." His fingernails allow that he was sick three times in the six months before he died and that "the last incident, two months before he died, lasted about two weeks." Of Jesse's case, investigators write: "Efforts to retrace when and how Mr. Cook obtained the weapon used in the armed car-jacking in Rhode Island, in the armed home invasion in Warner, New Hampshire, and that eventually resulted in his death, have been unsuccessful to date. The firearm is a Heckler and Koch, .40-caliber semi-automatic pistol. The last known owner sold the gun on consignment in Louisiana. No further information has been obtained." The body of our ancient ancestor, on the other hand, understood as "a mass of citations," has enjoyed a kind of lavish attention whose labor knows no bounds, with results like the poetry-forming lists of all that was found in the proximity of his body: "chaff and grains of einkorn and barley," "seeds of flax and poppy," "kernels of sloes (small plum-like fruits of the blackthorn tree)." "Plants found amongst the Iceman's belongings support the study's portrait of an inquisitive, complex society," researchers write; they don't add, "as opposed to our own." "Birch polypore fungus" on his tools, bracken fern found in his stomach, and traces of bog moss all served medicinal purposes—evidently the Ice Man lived with a lot of pain that he spent a good deal of time medicating (not much has changed).

Like Jesse's, the circumstances of Ötzi's death were violent, but no one concludes that he was an outlaw undeserving of our regard. The Ice Man appears to have died from a combination pierce of an arrow to his left shoulder and a blow to the head, but what's even more astonishing is the discov-

ery of traces of blood from at least four other people on his
gear: one from his knife, two from the same arrowhead, and
a fourth from his coat. I love the precision of the narrative
that follows: "Interpretations of these findings were that Ötzi
killed two people with the same arrow, and was able to retrieve
it on both occasions, and the blood on his coat was from a
wounded comrade he may have carried over his back."

Of Jesse's tattoos let us note that they mostly were words—that
floated down from the typewriter, their paper, his skin. With
nothing left but Jesse's tattoos to go on, I will read them: "to
love me" is a poem; it's an elliptical, pregnant, fragment-phrase.
As if to say, "To love me, follow these directions. . . ." Or, it
aims to create a parallel aphorism, afresh, each day, along the
lines of *to love me is to* . . . fill in the blank; *to know me?* It's
a tattoo as a reminder to myself . . . to love myself. It could
just as easily say, "Don't forget to love me," inserting the ever-
longed-for "you." Or, "Remind me to love myself, You!" *To love
me, be here.* I don't think the wristed words want to be read
in tandem. The entire ensemble is an ode to incompletion.
Not "be here now." Not "be here or be square." Just "be here,"
but with a sense that something is missing, not lacking, but
TBD. Jesse's tattoos are fill-in-the-blank missives open to ques,
ques, question. The typewriter will fill them in, in time; it's the
way to being and becoming, it's the marvelous music-making
machine, not on a bicep but on a lowly forearm, the writing
muscle, not the fighting muscle. As for "Ques Paulson" tacked
above an elbow, he's an alter ego not exactly from another
planet but from another class. A dickey-wearing avatar whose
rooms smell of pipe tobacco and whose hair is plastered, his
sideburns elegantly, severely trimmed. He feasts on petits fours.

With nothing left but what transpires in a classroom, I have one of Jesse Cook's poems. On a day in the pain-and-its-unrepresentability class, I suggested we pursue meditations on the obverse of pain, on pleasure. Jesse wrote a list poem that began with the leading phrase, "my pleasure is . . ." followed by an ever morphing list of adjectives from "tomorrow" to "too poetic," "sold" to "blind," "bourgeois" to "clueless," "alone" to, in the final line, "*dead.*"

I still have my closing comments. In the page's middle distance, the suggestion in light blue ink: "Consider inserting the phrase 'my pleasure' at key junctures to create a more consistent yet ever shifting rhythm."

Following the last line, I had written: "Not the final word."

The author acknowledges the following sources: "Final Report Regarding Home Invasion Suicide, Warner, New Hampshire"; John Robb and Oliver J. T. Harris, *The Body in History: Europe from the Palaeolithic to the Future,* Cambridge UP, 2013; Mellan Solly, "What Otzi the Iceman's Tattoos Reveal about Copper Age Medical Practices," *Smithsonian Magazine,* September 10, 2018; as well as Wikipedia's "Ötzi."

The Red Parakeet

LINA MARÍA FERREIRA CABEZA-VANEGAS

The barking of a pack
of mongrel dogs and the
chirping of a red bird
inside a wicker cage
while the family sleeps.
Not soundly, but deeply.
The deep bruised sleep of
jungle heat and an army
base days, so the scarlet
screech of a scarlet bird
does not wake them.
Even as it flaps its wings,
as it flies from side to
side, as it chirps and
screeches and the sound
of mongrel dogs racing
toward the small house,
grows louder, and louder.
Everyone sleeps, everyone,
but the eldest girl.

Stop.
Try again.

"Oh!" My aunt says,
"Lina, I have some-
thing for you!" So, *Do
you?* I ask, and watch
her slowly pull out
her feet from under
the covers. Eight toes
on the bare floor and
her bare hand on the
valve of a bedside oxy-
gen tank. "You won't
believe it," she says.
"You really won't."

*The night is quiet, the
family is asleep, but the
blue bird is still chirping
in its cage. Still cawing
and screeching, still in
a fit of feathers and
flight, dashing from side
to side, back and forth,
again, again, while the
eldest girl tiptoes toward
the cage. She should be
asleep. In bed, out cold,
eyes shut. Ten fingers
and ten toes beneath
a sweat-soaked sheet.
But, "What is it?" she
whispers, as the chirping
comes to a sudden stop.
"What's wrong?" she says,
as the tap-tap-tapping of
metal-spoon beak strikes
the cage door. "Let me
out," it seems to call out
to her, "Let me out, let
me out."*

No.
That's not it either.
One more time.
From the top.

"It's somewhere around
here," she says, rifling
through pages, reaching
for shelves and balanc-
ing on absent toes.
And I imagine a black
forest fire foot. Gan-
grene and rot, a doctor
with a face mask and a
chainsaw yelling tim-
ber, cutting toes. "It
was just right here," she
says—cancer, chemo,
heartbreak, and time.
"I know it was," and
I watch my aunt con-
tinue to rifle through
notebooks and papers
with shaky hands. "I
set it out just for you, I
know I did."

*The night is quiet, the
family asleep, and the
silver bird in the wicker
cage doesn't sing anymore.
When they first found it
on the forest floor, with
a mangled wing and an
eye like a broken marble,
it made a thin sound
like cracks spreading
across sugar glass. But not
even that, not anymore.
Not since they crouched
around it and asked,*

"What's wrong with it? Will it fly? Will it die?" But they were only children then, and they only had each other to question and themselves to answer, so they all watched as the eldest girl picked up the dying bird and said, "Let's go home.

You know that
can't be right.
Think, Lina. Think.
Your notes.
Find them.

"Maybe . . . maybe . . . where is it?" I slide my hand over shelf and whisper, *Take your time.* A runway of dust and a flyaway finger finally landing on a black-and-white photograph of a man in uniform. My grandfather, my aunt's father, the colonel. The man who joined the air force mid-war, who flew out on a Sunday morning after mass, who pressed a button too late, who fell from the sky strapped to a faulty parachute. Who struck the ground of a chirping jungle with the bareness of cloth-wrapped flesh.

Decades later, I watch
his eldest daughter
flipping through pages,
pulling out books.
"Where did I put it?
Why can't I find it?"
And I picture her,
twelve years old on a
Monday morning, in
an air force base school
when she is pulled out
of class, when she is
told that it's over, that
"We found him."

*The cage is empty, the
family is asleep, and a
cocker spaniel whimpers
in the front yard while
the eldest daughter
dreams of crushed wings,
red feathers, and iron
beaks ripping her toes
from her feet like black
worms from the scorched
earth.*

"2011, sometime after
September. 115 total,
number 29, 30, and 31."
This isn't helping.

"I knew it! I knew I
had it!" My aunt pulls
out a clear plastic
sleeve filled with yellow
pages. "Look," she says,
"look," pointing at
old receipts covered in
cursive scribbles I can
barely read as she

places them in my arms, "Lina, look." Like a nest full of petrified eggs. "They're all here," she says, "all of them."

The dogs are black forest phantoms, but they are barking as if made of meat and bone, as if their mouths are filling up with blood. The cage is empty, but the birds are singing still, as if their feathers had never been plucked, their necks never snapped.

The family is still dreaming, though they hardly sleep anymore, and the colonel is tiptoeing through the house with cracked-marble eyes and mangled wings as if he had not been dead and buried for over a year now, while the eldest girl plays with the cocker spaniel in the front yard. While she asks her grandfather, "What's wrong with her?" Asks, "What is happening? Why is this happening?" When the dog opens its mouth and dyes the grass scarlet with poisoned blood.

"Dog kept barking,
meat likely poisoned.
'Not uncommon,' Aunt
says. 'Happens all
the time,' she says."

About the bird, Lina.
The red bird.
There must be
something. Find it.

"Lina," she says, "do
you see?" I flip the
pages over, I read the
receipts, water, electric-
ity, and coal, numbers
I barely recognize from
an economy before the
war. Ten pesos here,
twenty pesos there.
But, "No," she tells me,
"not that," and turn-
ing the pages over, she
points, "Here."

*"No, no," The eldest girl's
grandfather says as he
kneels down beside her.
"Don't worry, little one,"
he says, "don't worry." As
the dog whimpers and
pants. "In the university
veterinary hospital," he
tells her, "there are men
with face masks and
stethoscopes who can put
everything back together
again." So, "Don't
worry," he tells the eldest*

girl. "Don't worry, don't
worry." Again and again,
until he sees her smiling
back, and he repeats,
"There are men with
face masks who'll put
everything back."

12. The Tree That Sings

13. The Bird That Talks

14. The River of Gold

18. The Animal
Serenade

35. The Little
Frog Gloglogló

36. The Little
Duck Gloglogló

37. The Little
Cat Gloglogló

29. The Red Parakeet

30. The Blue Parakeet

31. The Silver Parakeet

"The Girl Who Sold
Her Soul to the Devil,"
I read aloud, and look
up to see my aunt's
face. A smile I barely
recognize, from a time
before the colonel,
before the cancer. Silver
thread and

colored glass. My beautiful aunt balancing on eight toes and a single smile. And all that hope wears her out and she has to sit down. "Churutumba the Bad Girl," I read in my great-grandfather's careful cursive, "Feruli the Good Girl," dozens and dozens of titles like orphaned limbs and severed toes. "The Red Parakeet," I read. "The Blue Parakeet."

The colonel is back inside his wicker cage and the poisoned dog back in the care of invisible doctors. So, "Don't worry," the girls' grandfather tells them. "That little dog will be back in no time at all. You'll see," he says, though the eldest girl has already begun to suspect, and he, begun to notice. So, "Don't worry," he repeats, and because he has lost his fair share of friends and family to tragedy and war, because he has heard the mangled song of broken wings many times before, he pulls his eldest granddaughter close, and he tells her a story

about a red bird. Then
he whispers, "This story
is yours and only yours.
I'll tell it only and always
to you." And when she
smiles he says, "Go on
then, bring me your
sister," and he tells her a
story about a blue bird
that is hers and only
hers, and then, "Go on,"
he says, "bring me your
sister."

38. *The Little*
Dog's Revenge

"Lina!" My aunt says
from the edge of the
bed, her eyes set upon
the pages in my hands
while she opens the
oxygen tank valve and
takes a deep breath,
"They're all right there."
And as I stare at the
titles I think, *There are*
men in face masks and
stethoscopes. I think,
Don't worry, don't worry.
Don't.

The girls' grandmother
pours waters on the red
patch in the yard and
watches blood slide off
of the blades of grass like
rain from silver feathers.
Years later the eldest
girl will find the only
ever-made record of her

grandfather's stories, and
balancing on phantom
toes she'll say . . .

". . . Lina! You can
write them, can't you?
You can bring them
back."

Unsightly

COLLEEN O'CONNOR

How was it that my lips were dirty?

I looked in the mirror and there were black and dark blue bits of what I assumed was grime stuck in the chapped creases of my top and lower lips. Not the corners, but the surface of the lips themselves—they were peeling and collecting dirt in the chapped, ruddy pink grooves that stretched and tore when I smiled. I grabbed some toilet paper from the bathroom stall but the flimsy tissue my workplace provided nearly evaporated when I ran some warm water over the balled bunch in my hand. I tried to make quick work of it—gathering a mound of paper, adjusting the faucet to a slow stream, listening carefully for the door. I didn't want to get caught cleaning off my lips with damp toilet paper because it seemed ridiculous to me— whose lips need scrubbing anyway? Whose lips become caked with the dark dirt of the city? Fingernails, maybe. The bottoms of someone's feet if she commutes in sandals in the summertime. But dirty lips seemed symptomatic of something much less common, of some flaw stemming from inside.

*

In my early twenties I developed a rash on my face that stuck around for seven years, a time during which I avoided mirrors and reflections of any kind in order to keep the rash out of sight, out of mind. I turned away from the sink as I brushed my teeth before bed. In public, I'd fixate on washing my hands in restroom sinks, my eyes glued to the foam oozing between my fingers, my glance steeled against the brunette reflection hovering vaguely in front of me. It became a point of pride after a while—my resistance to vanity so strong that not only did I not need to check myself in a passing mirror, I actively avoided it.

But the self is needy and not easily ignored. One day it came creeping up inside me like a weed until I found myself looking unabashedly and directly into a mirror, quite literally face-to-face with the dark circles under my eyes, the worry line cutting across my brow, and the red, scaly rash sprawling across my cheeks and around my lips.

I developed a skincare routine. I did hours of research on websites and blogs and skincare message boards. I stood in front the bathroom mirror, studying the sight just three inches from the glass, and I ran my fingers across every inch of my face, over every misshapen pore and fine line. I applied creams religiously, sometimes even waking in the middle of the night with the sudden horror that I'd forgotten to apply before bed, then scurrying to the bathroom to rectify my mistake.

Ultimately, I rid myself of the rash, but for every bump and scale I removed, a new wrinkle or dark spot seemed to appear. So I added another product to my routine. And I added another. I studied my face even harder and I researched new products, new trends to try. Serums, I thought, were the way to go. I'd likely been influenced by trends—at the time, serums were all the rage because they offered affordable ways to access the regimens usually saved for the wealthy. Brands popped up that promised inexpensive, *pure* formulas, free of the fillers and scents that the more expensive brands needlessly used to make their products *feel* more luxurious, to make them smell spa-like and fresh.

Typical, I'd thought. Luxury itself is a bullshit brand, silky to the touch and sold in sleekly designed bottles with hand-drawn fonts, priced to make one smell clean and feminine, priced to make one smell the way the wealthy smell, or the beautiful.

Though the wealthy and the beautiful are one and the same, really, or so I'd learned in my first three decades as an American woman. A few years earlier, as a young fundraising professional, I'd attended a meeting at our board director's high-rise office. He was a partner in one of the biggest law firms in Chicago, and when we cleared security and survived the three-minute elevator ride to his floor—not long in the grand scheme of things, of course, but an eternity for an elevator ride, which tend to be, in my experience, only a few inconsequential seconds—the doors opened to a lobby that looked like that of a sleek luxury hotel. Everything was white quartz, smooth stone that was somehow both shiny and matte. There were plants and fresh flowers, and yet it still felt businesslike and professional.

The most remarkable thing, however, was that it smelled inexplicably like fresh orange. I looked around for any sign of fruit, but there was none. All I saw was wealth, and plenty of it—designer suits and the red soles of fancy shoes whose brands I can't pronounce. That was predictable. The wealth I'd expected, and it didn't even intimidate me that much—I'd grown up around wealth, knew what it looked and sounded like. The smell, on the other hand, was unnerving. It held an exclusivity I couldn't put my finger on. We know you're not one of us, it seemed to say, and not even because of the balance on the ATM receipts littering the bottom of your purse. You're sloppy. You can hide the trash in your bag, the bits of paper and cigarette foils and gum wrappers, but your whole person is an intrusion on the very air of this place—its sweetness and the freshness that hits as soon as the elevator doors open.

*

There's wealth, and there's beauty, and there are the ways we lurch toward both, desperately trying to be good enough. But their markers are sneaky. Their trappings are so tight that unless you're already inside them, it's nearly impossible to find a loose spot, to peel a corner up for yourself and crawl inside.

I'd tried with serums. Face rash under control, I got adventurous. At thirty-five, I'd developed what the commercials call fine lines and wrinkles, and my skin seemed uneven, swallowed, and dulled. I thought if I put in the effort, I'd fix it. The effort is what matters. Commit yourself to a regimen and make your appearance a priority. Through study and determination, I too could be beautiful. I explored the qualities of different skin types—dry, oily, combination—and the different ailments a person might find on her face. The rash had likely been some form of dermatitis, which is less of a condition itself than it is a vague, catch-all bucket for all kinds of rashes and peelings. Skin, as it turns out, isn't very understood. I guess I'd expected to find clearly defined symptoms, a hierarchy of skin problems and their corresponding cures. For the most part, though, it was guesswork. Trial and error. I scoured message boards to read people's stories: They went to doctors and they tried a few creams, and not the luxury brand creams that promise youth and beautify, but creams branded as medical, clinically proven fixes for the sickness plaguing your face. I read about people burning their skin with acid-based treatments and desperately trying to replenish the moisture they'd burned away. Face washes caused hives. Rashes relapsed. Acne is its own personal hell, with nightmare photos and clear-skin endings that made me actually tear up. *This is my face,* I read over and over again. *I just want to feel okay when I walk out the door.*

✳

Some rashes last forever. My grandfather developed shingles in his nineties, which comes from the same virus that gives us the chicken pox. It seems cruel to me, devious even, that a skin virus we used to consider a rite of passage stays inside us, dormant, sometimes finding the right moment in time to break through the surface again, only this time significantly more painful and disruptive. The pain, I've heard, is excruciating— and not in the unbearable, unscratchable itch way the chicken pox is known for—but deep, skin-searing pain. It tends to affect only one quadrant of your body, an odd fact that makes the virus and its pustules seem even more intentional, more calculating. My grandfather went to his doctor and showed him the unsightly, painful rash spread across his left shoulders and chest, and the doctor prescribed some cream and recommended ibuprofen. When my grandfather went back four months later, the pox still oozing and crusting under his polo shirts, the doctor gave him more cream and the cold news that, because of his age and the tenacity of the virus, he'd likely have it for the rest of his life—a length of time that, as my grandfather pointed out, was likely not that long.

It astounded me then, that phrase: *the rest of your life.* I was probably twenty-five or so, not yet committed to anything, and I had always considered the body to be wildly unpredictable. Our physical selves change and adapt—we gain weight and lose it, our hair grows, we get colds and recover and our skin wrinkles and we fear cancer and if we do get it, the tumors grow and spread and we shrink them with radiation. But this—this was going to stick. A cluster of sores, restricted to the upper fourth quadrant of my grandfather's body, would stay fixed there forever, or at least until his body was gone. He could count on it for the rest of his life.

Even the face rash I'd had on and off for seven years hadn't ever seemed permanent to me. It came and went and was stubborn and disgusting—small patches of what began as smooth, inflamed bumps that quickly turned more sinister, breaking and weeping until they dried out and peeled for weeks at a time. The location varied—sometimes it would appear on the left side of my face, other times on the right, or, when I was very lucky, on both—but it generally began around my mouth, above my upper lip. I'd feel the bumps, they'd come to their heads, then the seemingly endless peeling began.

But despite that regularity, despite how predictable it was, each time the rash flared up again it felt like a brand-new occurrence, unconnected to the previous ones. As I researched skincare post-rash, I began to realize how silly that attitude had been. Of course they were connected. It's all the same rash, spread out over seven years of outbreaks. I'd been naive to think otherwise. But any realization of my own naïveté stopped short of an admission that the rash might come back—that, in fact, it probably would.

I researched skincare and I got arrogant. I emailed manufacturers. I bought three serums. I bought three more. They came in clear glass bottles with droppers and twice a day, morning and night, I squeezed the clear, viscous stuff onto my fingers and slathered it across my face and lips and neck. This wasn't luxury, it wasn't vanity—it was science. It wasn't the same as indulging in those fresh and floral scented rituals that beautiful, wealthy women use to engage with their own femininity and demonstrate their commitment to some vain superficiality. I was in my tiny bathroom, hunched over the cheap, faux-ceramic sink, applying serums with words like "2% hyaluronic acid" and "cold-pressed" and "high-spreadability" neatly printed on their black-and-white labels. This was my new self. I'd found a way to slip a finger under the tight trappings of beauty, to get a sneak peek at what it might look and feel like to be like one of them—committed to the effort of being beautiful or, at the very least, committed to untying that knot in my gut that seemed to tighten every time I walked out the door.

After a week, my skin felt soft and looked brighter. A week after that, all hell broke loose.

The rash was back, and with gusto, in a way that seemed to mock me. *What on earth were you thinking*, it said. *Did you really think you'd beaten me?* It was as if by simply paying more attention to my skin, by daring to try and care for it, I'd awoken the rash, reminded it not only of itself but of its hold over me, of its seemingly endless capability to bust through my surfaces and announce to the world that my face was not one to be beheld for too long. The bumps were small and red at first, contained to the right peak of my upper lip, and quickly the peeling followed. I initially (and naïvely) mistook it for dryness and applied serum directly to it.

Moisturizing serum. The serum that had made the rest of my skin look and feel actually dewy—a word I had never even considered applying to my own face. But this time it made everything worse and eventually the rash spread across the entirety of my upper lip, around my nose and onto my cheeks, then down my chin, jawbone, and parts of my neck. First the bumps, then the red patchy inflammation, the weeping, and finally, the peeling. It looked to me as though my skin was fighting itself—what was underneath trying desperately to come out, busting the existing top layer of skin to bits, tearing it and unhinging it until it dried out and flaked off.

Eventually, my lips chapped too, and as a result bits of dirt and grime stuck in their dried-out crevices. It was after all this that I found myself in my workplace bathroom, frantically trying to wet a mound of cheap toilet paper and scrub the grimy dead skin off my lips. I took a couple steps back from the mirror to see how obvious it was from further away, then a few steps forward. How close do we stand to other people anyway? I experimented with distances in the mirror over the sink, then in the full-length one hanging to its right. It was impossible to tell what was right. I've never conversed with myself, and anyway a mirror image isn't precisely what we see when we look at another person. How far away would a person be from this face when they wanted to talk to me? And what does that distance look like? The obviousness of my face—of its wrinkles and freckles and inflamed, peeling, dirt-encrusted skin—suddenly seemed utterly unknowable.

My mother used to tell me she could spot a European woman from a hundred feet away based on the quality of her shoes. *European,* I now realize, was code for *glamorous,* and glamour a particular type of beauty that, the way I see it, always implies unattainability. We call a woman *pretty* or *beautiful* knowing that there are others, likely in near proximity, who share those attributes. Beauty may be rare, but in a way the term is itself a catch-all for the myriad of ways women's looks are visually striking. *Glamorous,* however, elevates a woman. She's not just beautiful, she has an *air* about her. When she walks into a room, the room itself shrinks around her. It's a quality we can know like the backs of our hands, can identify from a hundred feet away, but once we've used it to describe someone else, once we've applied it to another person in a room, we've isolated her, withdrawn ourselves, and slunk ourselves down to the unglamorous. Why is it, I wonder, that my mother, a woman who had an eye and means for shopping, spent years refining her ability to identify a glamorous woman's shoes without ever attempting to purchase those shoes for herself?

My mother also tells a story of how, during the early 1970s, she went to a disco for the first time and got drunk on cocktails. My mother has always been more of a wine drinker, and the hard liquor made her head spin. She left her friends to find a bathroom, feeling confident in her above-the-knee, camel-haired, A-line skirt and knee-high riding boots, and wandered through what seemed to be a hall of mirrors looking for the ladies' room. When she finally found what she assumed to be the door to the bathroom, a woman wearing an identical outfit stood in front of her and, the way my mom tells the story now, she marveled at how stunning this woman looked. *Oh no,* she said to her, *you go first, I insist.* The woman, however, was also motioning for my mother to go first. *No you go. No, you. No, please, you, I insist.* This went on, she says, for some time, until she finally realized she was standing, of course, in front of a mirror.

What a lucky experience—to have seen oneself without any self-awareness, and to have marveled at that self. And then how painful—to come back into one's selfness and feel, inevitability, the sense of disappointment that comes so pointedly and specifically from the mirror.

When the rash reared its ugly, peeling head again after my first real attempt at skincare, I'd thought it typical, somehow representative of my inability to ever get anything physical quite right, some outward manifestation of an ugly, crusted inside. The more I tried to polish this facade, I thought to myself, the more obvious the blemishes both inside and out. I should have kept facing the other way when I brushed my teeth at night, should've studied my hands in restrooms instead of my face.

I was a fool for thinking I could partake in skincare, could incorporate some self-care ritual into my life that wouldn't just backfire and prove that this self wasn't, in fact, something worth caring for. I can try to hide the trash, the fact that I'm aging, the way I've never felt pretty, the fact that being feminine is something that has always felt just a little off to me, but my body would always remind me of what it's capable of. Its very presence constantly interrupts, ruins an otherwise perfectly fine day.

Colleen, my partner said to me when I lamented my failed attempts at skincare and the larger implications of the rash spread across my face. *It's something physically uncomfortable you have to deal with. It isn't a metaphor.* That was the day I'd been dabbing my filthy lips with wet toilet paper and bits of the flimsy tissue stuck in the cracks and creases. I wiped them with the back of my shirt. I listened carefully for the door. No one ever did see me doing it, but when I walked out of the bathroom, my lips still swollen and cracked but relatively free of that baffling dirt, I felt like I wore the whole thing like an ill-fitting jacket hanging askew off my poorly postured frame.

＊

As far as I know, my grandfather still had shingles when he died nearly a decade after his initial diagnosis. I'm not sure if he kept up with any kind of lotion or salve, if the pain bothered him (he was never one to complain), or if the added pains of aging—the brittle bones, dried-out joints, the Paget's disease he'd acquired, or the slow and steady dementia he watched steal away my grandmother—if all that eventually outweighed the searing pox on his upper right quadrant. If it became, maybe, a comfort, something he knew he could rely on for the rest of his life, however long that was going to be.

Those Were the Days

SONYA HUBER

The upscale outdoor mall in Columbus, Ohio, was called Easton, and I drove there with my baby son and a coupon I'd received in the mail for a free pair of cotton underwear at Victoria's Secret. Those were the days of public assistance, the days of finishing grad school and then working three jobs, the days of the gut-punch sickness at a hospital bill we couldn't pay. The days of phone calls and applications where we listed how little we had. Those were the days of scary, of a marriage riven with deep problems that I coated with loathing or sprinkled with hope that this would pass in time, that this was the hard part, and if we could just power through this rough patch, it would all be okay. Those were the days of leaving the house with the baby to sleep in a hospital parking lot because it seemed to be the safest place. I was thirty-three. These were not the fun days of my twenties scrounging coins for another beer in an Irish pub in Boston. These were the days of *how do I escape, how will I feed us,* and *all I know is that I will,* and that I, I myself, would have to find a way.

What's interesting to me is that I treasured the errand of going out to Easton to walk in the summer warmth toward dusk. It was Saturday, I think, but the place was deserted. My son would have been about nine months old, squirmy and healthy and dozy. And yes, fed with the grace of the coupons for Women, Infants, and Children who found that they could not adequately feed themselves. Likewise I had found that the state health care program rescued both of us when there was no other affordable option after I got pregnant. I have never been more patriotic than that year, and I know that if our nation gave more help, its people would return that care and devotion tenfold.

But anyway, I also liked to pretend. I liked to go to Easton and stroll, to imagine I was just a young woman at the mall, to pretend that my husband hadn't graduated the outpatient substance abuse program downtown and then relapsed and also received a mental health diagnosis that he doubted was true, so he often didn't take the meds. But those hard days were interspersed with the pearls of sobriety, so we were composed of terrible and hopeful together. And I was barely functional with fear, as jaw-clenchingly rigid as any child of an alcoholic might ever be once she realizes she's fallen into a generational pattern of the heart.

I went to Easton so that the white knuckles on my steering wheel would relax, so that I could pretend I would be back in the middle-class aura of my youth, the place my parents had fought to achieve, to the mall south of Chicago with its fountains and its food court, where I could buy a pair of earrings at Claire's and imagine that the kind of earrings I chose had a cipher-like ability to reveal the direction of my life. Even then I had wads of depression and healthy glowing slices of joy as sour-sweet together as lemon meringue.

I'd turned in my coupon for my free pair of simple black cotton panties with white piping and embroidered with a tiny pink poodle over one hip. The coupon said "No purchase necessary," though the idea was that you'd buy more. I did not. I took the beautiful pink-striped rigid cardstock bag with black fabric ribbons for handles, the panties wrapped inside in pink tissue. This bag could stand on its own, and its presence seemed to offer a bit of capitalism's glitter, its whisper that if you buy it in a mall, your life will smell as nice as scented candles. I was soothed, because I needed free things, and if you had one name-brand thing, it might like an incantation summon more, or summon the money needed to buy more. I was sated with my own thriftiness, proud that I had gotten a pair of underwear for free. I put the bag in the net container beneath the stroller and we wheeled out the door.

Out on the boardwalk of beige pavers, a young man approached with a clipboard, and I was uneasy, because it was to be the kind of sales interaction from which it was difficult to detach. There was no crowd to disappear into; I was his only prospect. I remember that he was tall and dark haired, long-limbed in a kind of rubbery way. He was selling maga-zine subscriptions so that he could raise money for a trip some-where—or something like that. He did the seamless thing they tell you in canvassing and sales trainings: *Let them hold the clipboard. Make them say yes.*

He promised me, I think, that all I had to do was hold the clipboard and let him do his spiel and he would let me go. He kept wanting to high-five me. Taken in by the disturbing rhythm of these space-invading sales tactics, I complied like a folded dollar bill. I was always an easy mark, always both uneasy and skeptical and then willing to go along because I felt guilty about my skepticism. *High five.* Our palms made contact, pure sales psychology, snaring me into a rhythm and rewarding me for non-accomplishments, the way large and small commitments start a numbing dance.

Somehow I was holding the clipboard and he was pointing to pictures of different magazines with stars and points next to them and the cost for each subscription. He needed a certain amount of points by tomorrow. The sheets with the pictures of magazines were laminated and worn, a bit of grime caught at the adhesive edges, and I found the level of wear disturbing, indicating how long he or someone else had been doing this.

"I really can't. I don't have—" I said.

His face loomed a bit closer. He returned to this created urgency—always the need, the deadline—which he restated to excuse the application of a little anger, just a bit. Somehow, now, I was letting him down, retracting something I had promised. Had I promised something? It was the contract of contact.

My son, used to the motion of the stroller and disturbed to be still, arched his back or squawked, and I felt that new tearing of attention that had made me a mother. I smiled placatingly at the young man and glanced, put one hand on the stroller handle and said, "I really have to go."

The young man's face collected a hint of intensity, and I remember somehow that his eyebrows weren't right, as if they had been all plucked off and were growing in spottily and penciled on in a line. I had a hint even then that maybe he was gay, that none of this story was what he said it was, and that he did have some sort of pressing need but it wasn't about points or magazines or a trip. I also sensed a chemical urgency in the way his cartoon friendliness turned so quickly to hostility, the flat black of his pupils.

I tasted an edge of fear, that edge of having a new baby that I was sworn life and limb to defend. Once I was just a girl who could tell this guy to fuck off and could swipe with a bristle of keys then run with my fleet feet, flipping him the bird with my hair flying. I stepped away and put both hands on the stroller. "I can't buy magazines. I have no money."

He scoffed. One magazine was so cheap, he said, the cost of a few cups of coffee. *Nothing to you.*

"Look—" I said, wanting it done. "I'm on welfare. I have no money. I'm leaving."

The memory that sticks with me, as if I have created it. It is as if I invited his rage, always my fault, which erupted on the sidewalk as I fast-walked with the stroller, now jogging, glancing into the Bath and Body Works to see if anyone was inside. He yelled down the long open plaza after me.

"You're not on welfare! Look at that bag in the stroller. You even bought something—You're a liar!" A pause. He wasn't following. He continued to repeat the word *liar.* Then: "You're disgusting!"

What I think about now, and part of what rends my heart, is the fact of passing and being invisible. So many people can't sense where I've been, and I pass as easily upper-middle-class, always a professor, maybe until I open my mouth. I think about the privilege that I signaled then and broadcast now: teeth straightened by braces, college-girl squint, an elasticity to my skin that bespeaks vegetables and not too much hard work outside or in harsh environments. Fear and authority both lodge in the body, and I have a little of both.

I think about how I was both telling the truth and lying. I wasn't lying: The facts of my life were true and unenviable. But I also knew that I wouldn't stay at that level of desperation. More pointedly, I knew I would do anything to escape because I knew exactly where I wanted to go. Where I wanted to go did not include crying to the point of vomiting when your car broke. I had a sense that I was entitled to a future, and that entitled desperation would make me ask for raises, make me apply to jobs that scared me, make me stay at awful jobs: because there was no other choice. I also had a security net, parents who could loan me car money and who would take me in with no questions asked. My little totem from Victoria's Secret meant a brief respite from my dollar-store life.

But it also meant so much to me because I was down with free shit, and at that point most of my pride had been busted out of me. No, wait: That's a lie. It would take longer, longer for me to admit how much I was suffering, long enough to really get help and say that I was scared. It would take longer to stop keeping secrets out of pride, to stop making do.

For a long time afterward, through the years of single motherhood and the harder years before the divorce, that moment of being yelled at in a public place was a tiny measure of my ability to be honest, even if it was a tiny truth dropped to get out of a coercive sales interaction. I had told the truth. And it was true: Things had gone awry, this was real, and I couldn't wish it away. When I'm uneasy, in the middle of conflict, at meetings at work, anywhere, the weird mantra that slips out of my mouth even now is, "This is real. This is happening." Because at any time, I might forget. I'm a good liar, and I'm an easy mark. I believe any story I tell myself.

At that moment, I was afraid of that young man and afraid for him. I wonder about that young man's life, and I think he was more desperate than me. And I have a feeling, just a guess, that he is no longer alive. I have a feeling that even as he scoffed at my poverty and attempted to sell me a pointless bundle of glossy content about decorating or sailing or makeup, that he was in the grip of a kind of trap borne of desperate decisions and limited options that had rippled out through multiple generations. I could sense it somehow in the skin of his eyebrows, in the way he sweated and the hollow in his eyes.

It is equally possible that the chemical-fueled hyped-up loathing he spat at me was the loathing of a young man who doesn't know at all, who has a picture in his mind of what "poor" looks like and he hates that picture, and that loathing is fuel for his whole life, is part of the sting that makes his drugs and his stupid choices so pleasurable, because he would never sink so low as to be a poor woman in her thirties with a baby in an outdoor mall where she cannot afford to buy a single object sold in any of the stores. This was the awfulness finally out into the open, the snickers and doubts of bosses, the hey-baby of random dudes. This is happening. Stop freezing when it happens. Run. Fight. I urge myself in that scene to grow the backbone I will need. I know it's coming. It's a slow movie. The main character takes so goddamn long to change.

I wonder if he ever felt like hell for that afternoon, or whether he even had time to grow into realizing how shitty he'd been. Maybe I am wrong, but I think that we were just kin enough for him to see the difference and the shared desperation between us.

Morgue

PAUL CRENSHAW

The day we found the morgue Dee said we were all going to die. We lived at the time on the grounds of an old tuberculosis sanatorium, where we obsessed over death. This was 1981, and most of the buildings were boarded over. What few remained open had been converted to homes for the developmentally disabled, which meant that all day, while we looked out the windows of our houses, we saw the residents wandering around the manicured lawns with their mental disorders, and all night, as we tried to dream ourselves elsewhere, we heard them calling to one another like ghosts.

The whole place was haunted. It had been built a few years before World War I, when tuberculosis was ravaging the country. After the war its halls filled with soldiers who caught TB in the trenches. For twenty years they wasted away in little rooms staring out the windows. In 1941, as bombs were falling on Pearl Harbor, the Nyberg was built, a hospital half a mile long, it seemed to us in the early '80s. By that time there was another war going on, this one in the air above our heads, and we called it Cold. Missiles and transmissions were flying over us at all times, and at any time, we thought, could come crashing down.

Maybe this morbidity was why we went to the morgue. We had heard rumors that nuclear missile silos were housed beneath the hill, and though I don't recall whether it was all the bombs we saw on the nightly news or the buildings themselves that caused us to believe such a thing, I do recall that around Christmas maintenance put up a giant Star of Bethlehem atop the Nyberg, like a signal we should follow, so maybe we thought we would find beneath Bethlehem something that would save us. I'd say now we were only kids, exploring our world like kids everywhere, only our backyard was an old sanatorium instead of a suburb. Instead of bake sales we had boarded-over buildings, and instead of Boy Scout meetings, we sought out the old morgue, beneath which nuclear missiles were said to be waiting.

From our houses we crossed a small creek and went over a dew-wet field behind Dorm One, Dee leading, Brock behind my brother and me. There were four dorms, but only One and Two were still open. The others stood like stones, eyes blacked out by boards, shutters sagging or gone altogether. Past Dorm One we crouched in the shadows of the pine trees until the coast was clear, then crossed the street running in front of the Nyberg and washed up against its walls.

Dee, whose uncle worked maintenance at the institute, said the door to the morgue was never locked. Still hugging the stone side of the old building, we ducked beneath the overhang where hearses used to dock to bring out the dead in the tuberculosis days. The door was indeed unlocked. Dee turned the handle. We waited in the darkness for our eyes to adjust and I'll say now I was more than a little scared, though I don't remember if I was scared of what we might find or of getting into trouble, as if I already knew there were things the adults of our world didn't want us to know.

A long hall led to an antechamber where faint light gathered sourceless around us. Already Brock, a year younger than we were, which meant he was eight or nine at the time, wanted to go home. I'll say I did too. Old equipment stood everywhere: tables and gurneys and steel sinks unstuck from the walls. A metal bed with wooden legs tied on it. In one corner crumbled tiles that had fallen from some other ceiling.

There were words spray-painted on the walls of old lovers proclaiming themselves forever together. Cigarette butts and beer bottles said we weren't the first to come here since it had closed. Most of the doors had been removed and a cold wind whipped down the halls and the building above us moaned as if it held within those who had once walked here.

I don't remember how long we rummaged through the rooms, nor what we were looking for, but I do remember finding storage coolers that had once held corpses, and drainage tubes for embalming. Old cabinets full of brown bottles meant to prevent death or preserve bodies. Machinery more medieval than medicinal. Long silver implements Brock said were to pull out brains and other body parts, so I suppose we were seeking death in the way morbid curiosity surrounds kids still coming to terms with life. That all our understanding comes from discovery, even if our findings are forged out of fear.

After sifting through the old discarded debris we saw at the back of the morgue a sign that said Bomb Shelter. I still don't know if there was a separate bomb shelter in the building, or if the sign meant the morgue was where we should go if the missiles ever flew, but we knew upon seeing it that the threat we'd heard about was real. There may not have been a missile silo beneath our shoes, but the Cold War was as real as the morgue, as cold as the bodies of those once embalmed here. I knew from my father watching the nightly news that the SALT II talks, limiting the number of ICBMs on both sides of the world, had just failed. The Soviet Union had invaded

Afghanistan. I was terrified of fire, and it came to me then that here was where we would hide if the bombs ever fell, under a building where thousands had died with disease in their lungs, unable to breathe, in a room where their blood was drained through tubes and their bodies embalmed so they could be buried.

"We're all going to die," Dee said, voice pitched like a late-night murder movie, and we all laughed, though I saw more than one lingering look back at the sign and the silver implements and the spray-painted names, as if we would remember it all forever.

It was cold when we came out. The dark was starting to set in. A line of cars was heading down the hill with their headlights on, like a funeral procession, and standing in the light of the Star of Bethlehem, I saw the leaves on the trees lifting in the first hint of wind.

That night a storm came up out of the west. A warm front had moved in to clash with winter's cold, and on the TV weather warnings lit up the state of Arkansas like radiation. As the wind started to rise, my mother took us to my grandfather's storm shelter, where we sat in a little room beneath the earth in the light of a kerosene lamp while the storm shook above us. All through the night our shadows stood on the walls. Each crash of thunder convinced me something was coming, so to soothe my shaking my grandmother sang some silly song. My mother smoothed the hair back from my forehead with a warm hand. I can still feel it there, soothing away all the scared. I never told her about the morgue and the bomb shelter and how scared I was sometimes, but she knew in the same way she sometimes sat out on the front porch smoking in the last light, some unnamed worry she carried around eating at her.

Twenty years later, when my daughters were little, they often woke crying. A spring storm would come up sudden as the end of the earth, and they'd flinch in each flash of thunder.

My older daughter was born during the civil wars in Afghanistan and Iraq; I sometimes rocked her to sleep while watching the nightly news. My younger daughter was born barely a year before two airplanes hit the Twin Towers like missiles, shortly after which the US invaded Afghanistan and Iraq. The world was either for us or against us, our president said, and some nights, when everything seemed to be circling back to bomb shelters, I stayed awake wondering how anyone could sleep. We were living in a basement apartment then, and when my daughters woke in the night I sang to them some silly song.

Forty years after the morgue I live in the Midwest, in a city where a movie about the end of the world was once filmed. I sleep in the basement when storms come out of the west, and flinch in each flash of thunder. The US is still in Afghanistan. In just the last few weeks, the US pulled out of the Intermediate-Range Nuclear Forces Treaty which had stood for over thirty years. Russia followed suit, and within three days, both countries had fired missiles into the sky, like a warning, or a sign. Sometimes now I wake in the middle of the night, wishing for a warm hand on my forehead, for a song to soothe me back to sleep. The basement is cold as a morgue, and I sit there in the darkness until the storm moves off, until I can breathe again, until I'm certain I won't be buried.

Fire

ALYCE MILLER

On a drizzly November morning, my mother entered the room I shared with my younger brother, and announced she had something to tell us. A terrible thing had happened in the night while we were all asleep. My friend Lucinda from around the block was gone. She had perished just after 11 p.m. in a blazing house fire that also took the lives of her father and her older sister Kayron. But another family member had also died: their English springer spaniel Duchess, the beloved brown and white dog who routinely made clandestine evening visits to our house and whom I unbashedly adored. Burned in her bed, the reports said. She'd never awakened. Lucinda's three older brothers and mother, with the help of heroic neighbors and, later, thirty-five firemen, managed to leap from windows and climb down ladders, while her father, a pediatrician, in one early version, had run to the girls' room only to be overcome by smoke, but corrected in another, was actually found dead next to his own bed. In the confusion of that flame-ridden night, stories and rumors emerged with one haunting image recounted in all the papers. "One of the little girls (Lucinda) was inside burning and I helped firemen carry her out," reported a university student passerby who was one of the first on the scene.

The fire, our mother explained, was blamed on a spark— *just a spark!*—that leapt out from dying embers onto the carpet in the recreation room where the family had been celebrating Lucinda's birthday. Reports were quick to underscore the irony that firemen found the protective screen meant to shield the embers propped up, useless, against the blackened wall beside the fireplace.

I was five. Lucinda had just turned six.

We had moved the fall before from Zurich via brief stops in two other states, to the tiny University Street rental, near Michigan's campus where my father taught in the music department, our house sandwiched in by Mrs. Howard's boarding house on one side and a dental office on the other, with a large fraternity house just behind us across the alley. This was back when young children and dogs roamed freely, when curiosity beckoned us into mysterious kingdoms of imagination and adventure, danger a negligible byproduct of our restlessness. Through the fence we'd peek at Mrs. Howard's middle-aged daughter sunning herself in a bikini in their backyard, and from our darkened bedroom window at night, we spent hours after our mother had turned out the lights, spying on the man who rented the upstairs floor and frequently entertained lady friends into the wee hours. Down two doors was the duplex with the two tiny Turkish boys, who often ran half-clothed out into the yard with their mother chasing after them, and next to them lived my friend Sheila, whose mother, aware of the vulnerability of her black child, ordered her directly home from school to lock herself inside and answer the door to no one. They lived in fear that Sheila's estranged father would come back to steal her, but that didn't prevent me from pushing open the heavy outer door and climbing the steep stairs to their silent second floor, half-expecting the father to jump out of the walls. Some days I was successful in convincing Sheila, by whispering through the door, to come out to play. Once her mother caught her and beat her, and I learned not to tempt her mother's frightened wrath. Curiosity drove me to wander farther than I was allowed, partly in search of interesting adults to introduce myself to. There was the beatnik sculptor and his artist friends, and the Indian writer in a beautiful sari, who after talking to me, became good friends with my mother. There was the lonely teenage mother who invited me inside her stuffy apartment to watch soap operas while she ironed, and who offered me my first drag off a cigarette. Events in childhood tend to strike one unnuanced note after another, before time and other losses, along with that backward glance over the paths we've taken, add the harmonics and the melody. Childhood's adventures are not easily separated from the dangers, though adult warnings seem foolish and uncomprehending until they aren't.

It was on our busy street, thick with traffic and pedestrians, that I defied my mother one day by running out between two parked cars only to collide with the bumper of an oncoming car. Brakes screeched, traffic came to a halt, while simultaneously my mother was yanking me hard back into the front yard. In what must have been sheer relief, she dressed me up and down for trying to cross without permission. No, it didn't matter that an older girl across the street had summoned me from her porch on the other side or that I thought I could sneak across and back before anyone noticed. *You should never have crossed alone—ever. Don't you know that children can die.*

I didn't. My mother sank to her knees, holding me close. She clung to me with only the certainty of that moment, when, brief as it was, I was safe in her arms.

But in spite of the close call with the car and the train I had once slipped under while we were on our way to the ship in France, just before it was about to leave the station, I remained bold with a child's confidence in invincibility. Sure, I fell off my clip-on metal roller skates and scraped my shins on tree trunks, and had to run fast once from a man who tried to lure me away, but I didn't understand my mother's agitation, which seemed to signal larger dangers of which I was yet unaware; a knowledge that often etched itself in her face and led her to issue warnings of what we should do "in case."

Which is maybe why, after the fire, when my mother walked my brother and me down to witness the charred remains of the house, I wasn't equipped to make sense of it all. We didn't take the alley shortcut, but walked the full block behind us, as if to acknowledge the somberness of the occasion. We stood there in silence, observers of unthinkable tragedy, while to my mind it seemed that the whole family had simply vanished. What had been Lucinda's elegant two-story white frame house rising majestically from a wide green lawn was now a wrecked, soaked mess of scorched walls and blackened timbers, the yard a pitted mudhole. The stench of wet ash lingered in the air. Memory tells me I stared a long time, but what emotions I called on that day I can't say. What was impressionistic then would yield a sharper focus over time, as understanding evolved, and the weight of the losses joined subsequent ones in my life. What can you really understand at five? Just enough to know I wouldn't see Lucinda and Duchess again. And to assume in some twisted logic that maybe it was normal for houses to burn down. Or maybe enough to be puzzled and to later merge Lucinda's burned house with the smoky stench of rubber tires someone burned back in the alley one summer night, the smoke and foul stench rising through the air. As days and weeks passed, I asked my mother repeatedly to talk about the fire and pressed her as to why Lucinda and Duchess hadn't gotten out of the house. How was it that the brothers and mother survive, I wondered, but the father and the two girls and Duchess didn't?

*

Lucinda and Duchess were gone. Lucinda remained fixed in my mind as an ordinary little girl with a bob cut, in a light-colored dress and white socks and black shoes, who floated away, unharmed, into the clouds. Duchess must be with her, or nearby, because sometimes I would feel her mildly musky breath in my face, or her thick fur against my body as we curled up together on the living room floor. Only over the years as other deaths close to me accumulated, a few of them quite terrible, was I able to imagine my way inside Lucinda's house that night, to understand the panic of her mother when she awakened to the smell of smoke, and the family's sheer powerlessness in the flames' fury. And how Duchess, the consummate dog of dream and fiction, had likely been overcome with smoke, and never made it out of her bed to save Lucinda.

Like most early childhood friendships, Lucinda's and mine was forged in the simplicity of proximity and age, one of several first gambles with intimacy. Surely we would have taken turns doing flips over the metal stand outside the dentist office on the corner, and practicing cartwheels in the alley. Did we ever walk home from school together, crossing busy Washtenaw by ourselves as unaccompanied children did then, and did we skip rope, or jump hopscotch? Was Lucinda actually allowed at my house or was I the one allowed at hers? When I met Lucinda, we had lived in the US for little more than a year. My American parents had spent two years in Rome and then five more in Zurich, where my father was lead tenor at the Zurich Opera House, and when my brother and I were born, we lived in a tiny apartment near the Zurich See. Our life there had been simple but my parents had missed out on seven years of life in the US. So when I first started kindergarten, it quickly became clear just how different we were. We didn't own that great American staple, a television. My parents often spoke in German and Italian to each other, especially when they wanted to keep things from us. Our house was full of books, and my mother spent long hours reading to us, even after my sister was born. My father practiced in the house with my mother accompanying him on the piano. We did not own a car, until my parents finally bought a very ancient gray Dodge we nicknamed "Mousie," which had a small hole rusted in the backseat floor. "Stay away from the hole," my mother would remind us as she put Mousie in gear, and we rolled around seatbelt-less in the backseat. I began kindergarten with no knowledge of Saturday morning cartoons or popular TV shows, which caused other children to poke fun and ridicule my ignorance. I confused a Huckleberry Hound stuffed doll someone gave me with Yogi Bear, and was laughed out of my first grade show-and-tell. My parents were unusual people, a bit eccentric, and unlike other children's parents. They were frugal because they had to be, but also philosophically shunned the postwar materialism that gripped America. We weren't exactly poor, but my parents were rebuilding a life, and in the eight years they had lived overseas, the world back home had changed. My mother was raising us as she'd been raised a generation before.

I don't recall how Duchess's self-initiated visiting routine began, but I don't remember her ever not being there. One of us would hear her paws thump across the front porch, and another would call out, "Duchess is here!," which was the signal to whip open the door and slip her inside. She was a loving, sweet dog of gentle disposition, who seemed to enjoy music as we all did. My father often practiced in the evenings, and she was content to lie under the piano with me while I sucked my thumb and stroked her fringey paws. In those hours, Duchess belonged to me, my first dog love, our bodies sleepily assuming the same shape on the floor under the piano. It was just before bedtime, when the street had gone quiet and darkness was settling outside, and we were all together, with Duchess at the center of our family. But time passed quickly, and the peace would be interrupted by Lucinda's oldest brother Mars's voice cutting through the night air: "DU-chess! DU-chess!" The sing-songy summons I claimed never to hear and begged my parents to ignore.

"We can't," they'd say. "Open the door and let her go." And even with the regret of her departure into the night, we delighted in the guilty secret of sharing a dog with the Edwards family.

I came to believe Duchess really belonged to us and we to her. The way her slightly mournful brown eyes gazed directly back into mine, while I tenderly touched the sprinkle of dark freckles dotting her white muzzle, which for some unknown reason I referred to as "mercy spots." This made Duchess officially a "mercy dog." For my sentimental father, she was the incarnation of his cherished childhood cocker spaniel Freckles he'd had as a little boy, a gift from an admiring fan who'd heard him sing on the radio when he was four. His family was too poor to properly vet Freckles when she became sick with distemper. An older brother had her euthanized without telling him. When he learned of it from a neighbor who called out from his porch, "Hey, they had to put your dog down today," he encountered a heartbreak he carried into adulthood. Needless to say, he was smitten with Duchess. Even when she wasn't around, Duchess was often a topic of conversation: Duchess did this and that, as we looked forward to her next visit. On nights she didn't make it to our house, my heart was sore with disappointment. There was always the fear she might not return. But then she did, loyal to a fault.

I was sworn to secrecy about Duchess's visits because, for some unexplained reason, my parents were convinced the Edwardses would disapprove. But now I suspect it might have had something to do with the family's affluence that separated us in ways I didn't quite understand. Lucinda's father, Dr. Edwards, operated his medical practice out of an office in their home, and so it was rare I was invited in any farther than the kitchen. I don't remember seeing Mrs. Edwards much, though when I did she was perfunctorily cordial but busy with her husband's business. It turned out Lucinda was lucky enough to have two mommies, one brown and one white. I had no concept of "maid." My own mother wore an apron in the kitchen and cooked food just like Lucinda's "brown mommy," and the other one, the white one, I saw only in the distance. The "brown mommy" gave us snacks and even once promised to take us to the movies, which I took to heart, having been to the movies only a couple of times in my five years. I was raised not to ask adults for favors, so waited patiently for Lucinda's brown mommy to set the date. Time passed. The movie trip was never mentioned again. When I asked my mother, she gently explained that often adults promise things to children with the best of intentions but can't, for one reason or another, follow through. It was a huge disappointment, but one I kept to myself. Then, from the newspaper accounts of the fire, we learned that Lucinda's "brown mommy," who remained conspicuously unnamed, had been spared by good fortune, both her own life and the tragedy of the family she'd lived with that fateful evening. It was, the *Detroit Free Press* reported, "the maid's night off." I didn't know her name and I never saw her again.

Over the next few days my mother read updated details about the fire from the newspaper. Mrs. Edwards had been roused by the smell of smoke, but was reluctant to waken her tired husband immediately. Instead, she went downstairs to check on the source of the smoke. But by then it was too late. She ran back upstairs to warn the others but was overtaken by smoke and collapsed by a second-story window, where she was pulled to safety by firemen. Later, she was sent to the hospital to be treated for shock. The three boys were able to leap from bedroom windows, their falls broken by some of the spectators that crowded the scene. Another report credited the neighbor who arrived before the firemen and ran a ladder up the side of the house for two of the boys. It took all thirty-five firemen working for over an hour and a half to get the fire under control.

According to the fire chief, "It was a big one. The whole rear end was an inferno when we got there. We couldn't get in."

My mother used the Edwards tragedy as an object lesson, stoking in me a lifelong fear of fireplaces, particularly since later, after a couple more moves, we would live in a house with two. Invoking what happened to the Edwardses, my mother guarded fireplaces like a hawk, sitting up into the night until the embers had gone cold. I habitually absorbed her cautionary tales into my own anxious little soul. If we ever smelled smoke we should *never* open our bedroom door without checking first to see if it felt hot. And if it was, we were to climb directly out the windows. This new dread joined my earlier obsession with being kidnaped, likely inadvertently instigated by my mother's recounting of the Lindbergh baby's fate, an event that had shaped her own childhood. What I once heard as the scrape of the kidnapper's ladder against the bedroom window ledge in the dark of night was now eclipsed by plumes of smoke, smelling like those rubber tires burned in the alley behind us. First came the heat of fire blasting against our bedroom door, then the race to knot our sheets together to launch ourselves out the window. There would be nets below, I was sure, and firemen waiting to catch us.

After a while the fire became a distant memory, because of course life goes on, as it always does. My father was often away, performing, so for periods of time it was just my mother and my brother and me (until more siblings eventually appeared over the next few years). During the months my father sang with the San Francisco Opera, the three of us he'd left behind developed our own habits and routines. The arrival of the evening newspaper meant my mother reading us the Jackson Twins comic strip during a period when the girls were imperiled. Then before bed, there were the books my mother would read to us for hours at a time. I missed my father terribly, especially at night when I would cry softly to myself in bed, and in his absence, I became protective of my mother. We were all aware of the terror friends of theirs had experienced when the husband, a professor of campanology, who had been out of town performing, unexpectedly returned a day earlier than the date the paper had announced. In the night he and his wife were awakened by a sound, only to discover an intruder emerging from their closet with a pillowcase over his head. This was the notorious "Pillowcase Rapist," who habitually tracked public announcements to determine when a woman might be left home alone. That night, chased by my parents' friend, he fled their house, eluding capture. Unnerved, my mother asked the local paper not to publish my father's trip but they ignored her. During that time, she was extra vigilant, getting up in the night to wander through the house and recheck the doors. A friend in the theater department loaned my mother a stage gun, which she kept in the top dresser drawer in her room. She showed it to me once, making clear it fired only blanks. None of this struck me as particularly odd, since in my father's world, people (mostly women) died tragically and violently many times on the stage.

One night, some time after the fire, my mother opened the door to our room, and ordered us to get up. "I need your help," she whispered into the darkness, which automatically made me feel important. Still groggy, we followed her instructions to head downstairs, and report back if we "saw anything." She didn't specify what, just "anything." She waited at the top of the stairs in her white nightgown, holding the stage gun. It felt like a treasure hunt. What might we discover? The house was dark, but once my eyes adjusted, it was possible to make out the familiar shapes of furniture and the piano, then the dining room table, and the kitchen sink. *"Please open the closet door." "Anything in the kitchen?" "Check the basement." "Is the back door locked?"* And with each of our assurances we'd found nothing, she'd call back, "Are you sure?" After we'd checked the whole house, including the basement, we'd found nothing remarkable. As we came back up the stairs, she was still standing resolutely on the landing, ghostly in the white gown, the stage gun still in one hand by her side. She'd heard a noise, she explained, and thanked us. That was all. We went back to sleep. Over time the Pillowcase Rapist morphed into other bogeymen, both real and imaginary.

When we left Europe, we caught a ship out of France and, after a lengthy, grueling, green-faced Atlantic crossing, arrived in New York. At the time I'd been thrilled with the whole journey that carried us across all that water, and the cramped double set of bunk beds where we slept, labeled A, B, C, and D. According to our mother, she had caught the steward serv-

ing everyone unfiltered water from the ship's tap that made us
all wretchedly ill. I have no memory of that, and no memory
of how we got from New York to my grandmother's house
outside D.C., or the other relatives we stayed with briefly
in Maryland and Ohio. In fact, the experience of our ocean
crossing reprised itself in a recurring dream that would shadow
me well into middle age. It always began the same. I am walking down a long, dimly lit hallway to join a line of silhouetted
men in black fedoras and long dark coats, waiting to buy tickets at the counter. I am alone. I have no luggage. I am small.
The hallway seems to extend endlessly until the men vanish, I
now have a ticket, and am directed to take a sharp right turn
into the dark ship itself, where only small patches of moonlight overhead intermittently breach the shadows on deck. The
ship itself looks more like an old abandoned Spanish galleon, a
ghost ship. First comes the sound of water sloshing against the
hull. But before I can turn back, the ship begins to move, first
rocking from side to side, and then gaining speed as powerful
waves break over the sides. By the time giant plumes of ocean
water wash across the deck, seasickness overtakes me and I
awaken in sweat-soaked sheets, nauseated and dizzy. Over the
years I trained my mind to stop this vertiginous dream earlier
and earlier, until eventually just the sight of the long hallway
would put an end to it.

But not long after the fire, a second recurring dream took
shape. This one also followed me out of childhood and into
my various adult lives and in the many places I lived.

I am standing on the side of a thickly trafficked street like
the one we lived on in Ann Arbor. (Later, that street would
morph into the roads and freeways of other cities I called
home. There's an unexplained urgency to cross to the other
side, but no break in the traffic. Anxiety rises the more help-
less I feel. I try calculating the pace of the traffic, pushing my
hands rhythmically the way I once planned my entry vault

into a twirling jump rope. It will mean risking my life, but what choice do I have? Then, with just the subtlest movement beneath me, as if the ground has opened up I am being gently lifted upwards. Up, up, up, over the traffic and across the roar and fumes. By the familiar feel of the warm body and texture of fur, I recognize instantly I am safely astride Duchess's beautiful brown back, as if it were the most natural thing in the world. I bend forward to grab her scruff. There are the familiar mercy spots strewn like dark stars across the bridge of her nose, the crinkly-furred long ears moving in the wind. We soar gracefully over the road with astonishing speed before she delivers me safely to the other side. When I dismount I expect her to follow me wherever it is I'm going. But she has vanished as silently and quickly as she came, and I am alone again, destination unknown, but safe.

A couple years after I'd been living in California, my mother brought up the subject of the Edwards fire in a phone call. It was seventeen years later, and I was seized with an urge to contact Lucinda's mother, whose devastating loss I was finally able to comprehend. Worried that I might upset her, I wrote as carefully as I could, saying little about my own life which might trigger painful reminders. I ended by asking if she might have a picture of Lucinda she could send me, that I would love to have it as a keepsake. A couple weeks or so passed before I received a warm reply, in which she expressed happiness to hear from me, and promised a picture very soon. I waited. But no picture ever came.

When I eventually took off to make my way around Europe, and seek out the city of my birth, it was like going backwards in time. Memories of Zurich from childhood were patchwork, accompanied by the funny lilts of Swiss-German, the other children I knew in the kinderheim, our tiny apartment with the rubber plant, shopping at the market with my mother and her einkaufsnet market bag, my father singing at the piano, the time I sat in the balcony with my mother at the Stadt Theater to watch my father perform Mozart in a powdered wig. Certain views across Lake Merritt in Oakland had conjured up ghostlike images that I once believed were dreamscapes. But now they were linked directly to the Zurich See—houses stacked on hillsides above the stretch of water—the vistas that shaped my world from the start, the closing loop of strange, haunted threads.

So often in these returns to our pasts, there is always something missing, and one thing I'd forgotten until recently was a very peculiar incident that happened right before the fire, though its impact would only be recognized after the tragedy. A disturbing story made the rounds at the Episcopal church where both Lucinda's and my families attended. A couple weeks before the fire a Sunday school teacher had instructed the children in her class to draw pictures of their families and houses. A mundane assignment with crayons and construction paper took an uncanny turn. As service was letting out, the children scattered to find the adults, and the teacher collected the artwork, only to be brought up short by what one of Lucinda's brothers had drawn. It was odd, she thought at the time, but only after the fire when she went back to the church classroom to retrieve it did the full import of it strike her. Eerily, the little boy's drawing featured only his mother and the three brothers standing in front of a white house. Smoke and flames billowed out of the roof and windows. If I remember correctly, Duchess was included in the picture, and if so, this would have been the only error. How was it, everyone wondered, that Lucinda's brother had drawn this before the actual fire, before her sixth birthday, before she and her sister and her father had met such ghastly ends, before Duchess was discovered still asleep in her dog bed, burned to death? No one knew what to make of it all, but it was discomfiting to all the parents, including mine, who resisted believing it to be portentous, or that a seven-year-old had somehow plotted his family's demise. But everyone pondered the mysteriousness of it, and of course it defied explanation. A child's familiar stick-like figures—mother, and three boys, the orb of sun shining overhead, and the scrawled sweep of flames and gray smoke curling into the sky.

I now live on the East Coast with two elderly animals: a sixteen-year-old dog and seventeen-year-old cat, loyal companions and witnesses of my life. Even with all the animals who have shared my life over the years, there is a thick thread of sentiment that still connects me to the brown and white dog who habitually appeared on our doorstep in the evenings, and who lay with me on the floor, matching inhales in purely embodied moments of breath and heartbeat. She became my fantasy of a dog, my canine analog, a version of Lassie before I even knew who Lassie was. My gold standard for a dog, protector and friend, exalted then, and idealized and beloved through memory.

It's tempting to wish Duchess hadn't left our house that fateful night. If only my parents hadn't so obligingly opened the door to return her home when Mars summoned her with his rhythmic call into the darkness, "DU-chess! DU-chess!" If only I had been able to refuse and cling to her, to insist this be the night she stayed until morning. But we heeded the call, as we always did, because we knew with certainty that she would be back.

It's tempting to speculate why Duchess didn't awaken that night at the first hint of smoke, recognize the peril, heroically alert the family, and dash upstairs to carry Lucinda out through fire and smoke, the same way she has, throughout the years, rescued me from danger, and flown me safely to the other side.

At those moments I could almost believe that there never was a fire, that the Edwardses simply moved away, and somewhere Lucinda is living her best life as I am mine. My own world has been a jumble of joys, disappointments, setbacks, deaths, all the sea changes of time. As each decade of my life flips over to the next, the fact is, Lucinda has never aged, as I have, but remains a six-year-old child, stopped in time. And Duchess? In my imagination she is still running, maybe through a field somewhere, or down the alley heading to our old house where we are all waiting. Her ears are bobbing up and down. Her tongue hangs out in glorious joy. Her furry paws barely touch the ground. She is determined to find me as I am her. Duchess. My first dog. Sweetest friend. Dog of mercy.

The Death of the Dog

PATRICK MADDEN

This story will go its way simply, for Karina, who was there, tells me that some stories are best told straightforwardly, without embellishments or explanations, without the kind of long-winded philosophizing, the "getting lost in the branches," which is my wont. Some years ago, after we took our six children to Sauce, Canelones, just north of Montevideo, birthplace of none other than José Gervasio Artigas, Uruguay's failed founding father, all the more loved and praised, perhaps, because he died in exile, his dream of a united Rio de la Plata unrealized, so that he never had the opportunity to try and fail to adequately put into practice his ideals. After we took our children there, to Sauce, also the hometown of Karina's cousin and her family, whom we see so seldom, because we spend only brief vacations in Uruguay, after that, or in the midst of that, on our way home, we stood patiently on a corner by a bar at the town plaza waiting for the bus back to Montevideo. Meanwhile . . .

How best to get to this central moment, this *thing* I am writing about?

Suddenly . . .

Unbeknownst to us . . .

Up the street a short distance . . .

People around us were talking amiably, joking, recollecting, predicting. A guy in the bar was smoking a hand-rolled cigarette, flicking his ashes into an almost-empty tumbler. Across the street kids were playing tag, running jaggedly, jumping over tiny fences, grabbing trees to brake and slingshot off in new directions.

None of this do I remember very clearly. I have dreamed it, imagined it from somewhere close to memory, or composited it from the general scene that day, other days, from other places and times.

What I do remember clearly, too clearly, is the subsequent sequence of sounds: growl of motor, hiss of brake release, yelp of distress, explosive pop.

The first two did little to attract my attention, and became significant only in retrospect. But with the yelp, I turned quickly to my left, where in one glance, I took in the inevitable scene:

> La pupila archivó
> un semáforo rojo,
> una mochila, un Peugeot
>
> —Joaquin Sabina, "Donde habita el olvido"

A large gray and red bus inching slowly toward me, almost touching the curb; a brown and white medium-sized short-haired dog lurching backward, struggling for release but caught by its leash; a drab red rope pulled taut and shortening with the inexorable progress of the bus's right rear wheel. I apprehended in an instant what was ineluctably coming.

The bus was too far away, the windows too tinted, the driver too focused, the background too noisy. Though my whole being electrified with the desire to stop the unfolding scene, I was powerless to effect any change. Then, as the dog's head disappeared beneath the rubber, and its legs twitched, that sickening pop. The bus, heedless, as buses tend to be, continued to accelerate, inching slightly away from the curb, crawling past us, turning right, heading, ignorant, toward the highway.

Meanwhile, I had jerked my attention back to my children, noted their faces contorted in confusion or consternation, and pulled the youngest of them into my coat, snuggling their eyes to their father, away from the scene up the street. Karina, with a knowing glance at me, did likewise with another pair.

So this is the story I tell people, when circumstances lead to discussion of disturbing experiences: I once saw a dog run over by a bus, and it popped. My children were there, I say, and I'm not sure how much they saw or understood, but I understood it all in a flash before it happened, so that its happening was secondary, a realization of the nightmare I'd had a split second earlier. Then, once the act was accomplished, my horror was all the more frantic, as I sought to pretend that the day contained nothing out of the ordinary, to protect my children from the knowledge I now carried.

As our bus back to Montevideo rounded the corner toward us, I heard no cries of loss or dismay, saw no seeming owner disconsolate at the dog's death, only a hobbled old man shuffling across the sidewalk with a shovel. We boarded and paid, found seats together near the back, and I craned surreptitiously to watch the event's slow, sad resolution.

> The turn of the road carried the scene out of my eyes
> in an instant, and swept it into my dreams for ever.
>
> —Thomas De Quincey, "The Vision of Sudden Death"

Trigger Warnings

AMELIA MARÍA DE LA LUZ MONTES

When I think about my father shooting himself, Peter Duel's suicide is not far from my thoughts. One happened before the other. Peter Duel's suicide was front-page news in the *Los Angeles Times*. My father's suicide, three years later, was recorded in a police report, and, for a time, the subject of neighborhood gossip. Yet, I connect both, because Duel's death feels now like it was a portent of what was to come.

Peter Duel was my adolescent crush in grade school. It was 1971. I was thirteen and living in East LA while Peter Duel was a few miles away in Hollywood, enjoying success on the cowboy Western *Alias Smith and Jones*. Peter Duel played Hannibal Heyes. Heyes and his cousin, Thaddeus Jones, were on the run. They had decided to leave their Wyoming gang, asking the governor for amnesty. But since the governor was loath to bestow it, they were left to continually prove themselves worthy. Each episode presented a new challenge for Heyes and Jones: to use their smarts and physical strength to avoid unwanted trouble.

Often, I had to convince my dad that the show was worth watching. While I was enthralled, he thought the show was tedious. Some weeks I was forced to miss episodes because my dad's special boxing matches were scheduled at the same time. We were a working-class family lucky enough to even have a television, my father would remind me. Even when no other shows were of interest to my father, he still needed convincing to watch Duel. I would point out his smart and upbeat personality. In the most dire situations, Hannibal Heyes always remained positive. His quick wit charmed me, although at thirteen I was unaware that the writers of the show were to be thanked for that. They had created a humorous, wily character that even Peter Duel envied. In an interview early on, Duel noted how his character's ability to stay hopeful and sunny was something he aspired to. At my age, I would not have understood Peter was alluding to his own personal struggles. At the time, only his close friends were aware that he was suffering from addiction and depression.

On the first of January, 1972, the front page of the *Los Angeles Times* featured Peter Duel's face and the announcement that he was dead from a self-inflicted gunshot wound. He had been home with his girlfriend, Dianne Ray. Near midnight, he told Ray, "I'll see you later," before walking to the living room and pulling the trigger. The next day, I was a devastated fan girl, totally distraught, holed up in my bedroom. Usually when adolescent moods overcame me, my dad would ignore me. But this time, he wanted to talk. We sat together on the couch, and he waited for me to say something.

"I just don't understand, Dad. I don't. How could he have done this?"

"I'll tell you how," my father muttered. "He's crazy." I remember how he took his time in this conversation. He took a breath and more forcefully said, "Anyone who does this is crazy. Just remember that."

Three years later, my father did just what Peter Duel did. By then, I was sixteen years old. I did not find out from another family member. I did not get called out of school because "something had happened." I did not get a phone call. Like Duel's girlfriend, I was right there when my father pulled the trigger. At that moment, I did not know he had a gun in his right hand. He was sitting in the driver's seat of our car, which was still in the garage. He had rolled down the driver's side window. I was standing to the left of the car, telling him that Mom said it was getting late and that she'd be out in a bit. It was a Sunday in September.

September in Los Angeles is often very warm. Earlier, I had felt the heat sting the soles of my feet walking the length of the driveway to get the Sunday paper. We were supposed to go to church that day and Dad had been sitting in the car for what seemed like hours. I had been hiding as well, but in my bedroom, dreading having to put on church clothes on such a hot day.

All I wanted to do was stay in shorts and a T-shirt, barefoot. But Mom kept calling from the kitchen, wondering if I was dressed yet. When I finally changed, I went to the kitchen.

"Where's your father?" she asked.

"In the garage," I answered, remembering how odd it was for him to be sitting in the car long before we were to leave.

"What's he doing?" Mom asked as she turned off the radio on the kitchen table.

I watched her spread her hand over the tablecloth, smoothing its wrinkles. "I don't know," I answered.

"Go tell him we need to leave in a few minutes."

I went back to my room to put on my shoes.

We really didn't know what he was doing. We didn't know he had bought a gun weeks before because we never had any guns in the house. Later, my mom and I talked over and over again about when and how he had come to a decision to do this. We imagined so many possible scenarios.

When I approached the car, I felt how the garage was a little cooler than the driveway, but not by much. I remember hearing how my dress sandals clacked on the garage floor.

"Dad?" I said. He didn't answer. He seemed to be staring at the top of the steering wheel, or past the driver's side front window at the garage wall.

"Dad?" I sidled up to the driver's side of the car.

He turned to look at me. Something seemed strange, even eerily wrong. He didn't have his dentures on. I had never seen my father without his dentures. It alarmed me but I thought it best not to say anything about it, thinking that if I did say something, it would embarrass him that I noticed. Today when I think about it, I suppose that in the throes of what must be an exceedingly stressful and high-intensity moment, a plethora of details must enter the mind as a kind of distraction to reach for balance, for some kind of reasonable thinking. To this day, I imagine him holding that pistol in his right hand, feeling its heft, its smooth metal, scanning every inch of its design, and deliberating for hours how best to aim it before finally positioning it carefully just above his right ear. He must have taken a lot of time to prepare and one thing paramount in his reasoning was that taking out his dentures would avoid a possible ejection of teeth. Where would they go? They might shatter the car window and then Mom would have to pay for a car window replacement, an unnecessary expense. Maybe he thought about that. And so he went ahead and carefully placed them on the passenger seat, later to be found by Mr. Fernandez, who lived across the street, a Vietnam veteran, who later told me that cleaning the car of all the blood that got into the most minute areas of upholstery and car knobs and door hinges was traumatizing for him.

"But I wanted to do it," he said. "I wanted to do that for your father."

He had always respected my father, telling me later that he considered him an elegant man, the way he carried himself, the way he spoke in measured cadences. Seeing him like this was as bad as or even worse than some of the things he had seen and experienced in Vietnam because there, you expect such things.

But I'm getting ahead of myself. Let me place myself back to standing near the car where my father sat. I told him Mom was concerned that we were going to be late for church and asked was he going to back the car out of the garage? I reminded him that he'd been there all morning and we were wondering what he was doing.

He looked at me and mumbled, "Get out of the way."

I think he said it twice. Because he sounded so different without his dentures, the way his mouth seemed to swallow his words, the way the tenor of his voice smashed his directive at me, I was alarmed enough not to ask questions, to simply follow his order: "Get out of the way."

I turned to look at the driveway behind the car and every time I think of this, I see everything in slow motion: how I saw a tricycle near the driveway curb and how I thought to myself, "Well, I'll just get that tricycle out of the way while he backs the car out."

I took one step toward the tricycle, maybe two. I know I hadn't walked completely out from the garage when I suddenly heard two or three consecutive pops. They were loud, strange sounds that made me snap my head back to look at where my father was, and in looking back, I caught the moment when his head drooped oddly to the left. No sound from him. Nothing. I remember my heart racing, my mind in utter confusion. I was scared but I wasn't scared. I knew but I didn't know. I was shocked but also somehow calm. I keep thinking that I must have tiptoed up to the car.

"Dad?" I said in a small voice at first. "Dad?"

With each "Dad?" I stepped closer and closer until I saw what no one should ever see.

And that's when I remembered Mr. Fernandez. I jerked myself around to the end of the garage and screamed to him, but I don't remember if it was "Help me" or just "Help."

And maybe I wasn't screaming. Maybe I was waving my hands. Maybe I was doing both.

This whole time, Mr. Fernandez had been watering his plants in the front yard, the plants that bordered the front of his house. We looked at each other for a second before he forcefully threw the hose. The green rubber line lifted up and around him, a wild snake spewing out such a rush of water, making an arc that caught the sunlight, so much water going everywhere and Mr. Fernandez running across the street, running past me, into the garage, letting out such a low horrific moan at the same time that I could hear the front screen door slamming.

"Oh no," I thought. Mom cannot see this. She can't see this. I ran to the bottom of the porch steps, ready to block her from reaching the entry to the garage.

"What's wrong? What's wrong?" she repeated over and over.

I said nothing. I could feel my muscles taut and strong, blocking her. No way was I going to let her see this. I grabbed her flailing arms. I don't know if I said anything to her. All I remember is my strength overpowering her, how she acquiesced, her strength diminished, how she fainted in my arms. Did I drag her or lift her toward the house? Somehow I opened the screen door and brought her inside. I laid her on the couch and there she stayed the entire time while I phoned the ambulance, my sister who was living a half hour away, and my mom's best friend. And because my mother was very religious, I also called the priest, who ended up sitting next to my mom until very late. After the ambulance arrived, I kept going outside to talk with the ambulance attendants.

"Is he okay?" I kept asking, even though I knew. I knew, but I didn't, but I knew. "Is he okay?"

The attendants just nodded or looked down. One said he was sorry.

Soon a long dark station wagon appeared with the word *Coroner* on the side of it. The black sedan seemed to float past the front of the house where I was watching it, confidently turning into the driveway across the street, then backing into our driveway, parking itself right behind the car where I had left my father.

That's when I noticed police cars double-parking on either side of the driveway.

Suddenly the house was full of people. Some of the ambulance attendants had come in to look over my mom. I noticed each attendant and each police officer bending down just a little after opening the front screen door and entering. I had never seen such tall people inside our house.

One of the police officers approached me. He was holding a binder and what looked like official documents on a clipboard.

"You're a family member?"

"Yes. Daughter," I said.

He began to ask me a myriad of questions, every question asking me to give a minute-by-minute narrative of what exactly happened.

"Did you always have guns in the house?"

My answer was quick and decisive: "No. Never."

And then I remembered how the month before, Dad had wanted to go to the Big K store, a big-box store from the 1970s that later became known as K-Mart. I had to go with him because Mom had insisted he not drive alone. He had suffered a stroke eleven months earlier and was paralyzed on his left side. He could drive our car because it was an automatic. He could manage everything with his right leg and his right hand and arm, but his walking was painfully slow. He walked with a walker. Mom couldn't trust that he would be fine by himself. On that day, when we arrived at Big K, he stopped the car, turned to me, and forcefully told me I could not go inside the store with him.

"Don't you even think about coming inside the store to look for me."

It was a strange request. But since the stroke his demeanor had changed. His moods were unpredictable. I was sixteen. I didn't understand anything about strokes, what causes them, what rehabilitation is best. Sometimes I wonder if in the 1970s, the medical profession didn't know either. It seemed that way. After almost a year, I became complacent. Sometimes his moods and unusual shouting were frustrating. My mother dealt with it all by taking him back to the hospital and getting more drugs. At times, the meds would leave him serene and peaceful; other times I noticed his once-clear hazel eyes become glassy and cloud up. Still others would cause him to become uncontrollably shaky and angry. At first I was concerned and worried, even scared. Would he ever improve? Even when I asked the doctor, the few times I had gone with my mother and father, there was no clear explanation about his behavior other than the doctor seeming impatient with me, telling me to be patient. Months later, I began to sulk or shrug at Dad's odd behavior.

On this day, though, I obeyed him. The parking lot was massive, and he had parked far away from the other parked cars. He took out his four-pronged walker from the back seat, his good hand shaking. I watched him ambling slowly, placing the walker carefully in front of his good leg, taking a step, and then dragging the paralyzed leg along by swerving his left hip

forward. A half hour, maybe an hour went by. Finally, I saw
him with his head down, focused on the walker, slowly returning. He was carrying what looked like a lunch bag. That was
it. I wondered a little about all the fuss for one small bag, but
I didn't care enough to be very curious.

I just wanted to get home. When he reached the car, he
opened the trunk, put whatever was in that brown paper bag
inside, and slammed the trunk shut with his good right arm.

When he got in the car, he said, snarling, "Don't you open
the trunk, you hear me? You're not allowed in there."

I remained quiet. I was a sixteen-year-old who wanted to
go home, listen to music in my room, call my friends.

I noticed how the policeman was writing quickly as I spoke,
the pen zigzagging down the page. When I talked about the
trip to the Big K and the car trunk, he stopped writing.

"Just a minute," he said. He set down his work papers and
went out the door. Today, I imagine him going outside, opening the trunk of the car, and finding the paper bag. Perhaps
he found a small box of bullets. Perhaps. Were two or three of
the bullets missing? Were they the ones that made those two
holes on the garage wall? Once he returned, he asked me a few
more questions, but this part is all a blur. I remember the way
his leather belt held so many other leather pouches and key
fobs, plus a holster with a gun in it; how the blue color of his
uniform could be called indigo, and how the material seemed
thick and impenetrable.

When he turned to leave, I followed him outside and saw
that all the neighbors were out.

It was a small crowd assembled on the street and in our
front yard. I became angry and embarrassed. I felt exposed,
on display. I felt responsible to protect what was left of my
family. I had been raised to be circumspect, to keep family
business private. Suddenly a most personal and shocking event
was glaringly public and they were all there watching. I stood

on the front steps and looked at them. In my loudest voice, I shouted: "Go home! This is not a circus. There is nothing here for you to see. Go home. You should not be here. Leave us alone!"

I stared at them until I saw them lower their heads. One by one, they turned and left, including a friend I knew from school who was on his bike. He seemed to bow, then turned the bike around and rode away.

When I saw that they had gone, when I watched two coroner attendants push a gurney with my father's body inside a zippered gray bag on top, I doubled over with pain in my stomach and slowly walked backwards toward the screen door. I entered. The priest was still sitting there with my mother. He had put what looked like a cold compress on her forehead.

My mother's best friend was there too, holding her hand. I don't remember when she had arrived. About then, I went to a corner near the television, and sat on the floor. I rocked and rocked. It felt so good to rock and not think.

Home

YALIE KAMARA

I noticed it on a Wednesday morning, a few weeks after moving into my apartment in Cincinnati, the city in which I would be pursuing doctoral studies. Before sitting at my desk to complete some post-breakfast writing, I heard a hoot lilting from the air conditioner pressed between the window and its ledge. A *coo-OO-oo, coo-OO-oo* wriggled through the machine's vent and floated into the sunlit living room. A perceptible rattle followed. While it's true that I do not have enough aviary knowledge to even fit in a thimble, I felt confident in my panicked assessment of the situation: An owl had somehow gotten trapped in my air conditioner. I rushed online and typed in search queries relating to birds caught in tight domestic spaces and the animal rescue services in Hamilton County.

I landed on the Raptor Inc. website. The image of this creature looked exactly like what I wanted to believe was caught in my AC—a ruthless, wild-eyed bird of prey that would eventually use its metal-hard beak to crack the entire brick exterior of the building. I hungered for my situation to feel *this* dire;

I couldn't handle another one of my apartment issues being ignored. I called the nonprofit's number.

*

The Middleton Manor, my new apartment complex, was a sprawling ninety-year-old estate tucked at the corner of a long, wide, gaslight-lined residential street in the Clifton district. While a building of this age had noticeable deficits (no elevators, dishwashers, or air conditioner), my unit did boast a particular charm: well-preserved hardwood floors, a wall-length built-in bookshelf encased in glass, and an eat-in kitchen (though in all honesty, the nook could only comfortably sit a child for a meal or a time out-session). It was the largest apartment that I ever lived in, and my first with a balcony. I could never tire of standing on a balcony made from what I still consider to be one of the most exotic building materials: brick. Abundant as it is in these parts, brick has never lost its novelty to me. As a woman who had been raised in earthquake country, whole buildings made from what I once considered a hazardous material is still a sight to behold. Brick will always feel new—its texture, plenitude, and its hue, the color of drying blood.

As much as I tried, I could only occupy myself with the niceties of my unit for so long; each day came with a new set of issues. Loose electrical outlets all over the apartment, the presence of sharp broken tiles in the kitchen, leaky faucets, broken cupboard shelves, an invasion of stink bugs in my bedroom, an inability to run hot showers, and eventually (far beyond the temporal scope of this story) no heat during the polar vortex—there was no shortage of dysfunction. I began to ask myself questions that highlighted my misfortune—*How do cockroaches wiggle through obstruction? And what personality trait does it take for one to trail across your bed as you are waking up?* "Arrogance," a friend retorted. "Pure arrogance."

The accumulation of inconveniences was unnerving, but more than that, I was bothered by the unpredictable nature of my ordeal—I had no way of knowing exactly how or when my living space would become further dilapidated. I didn't know what awaited me.

✳

"Raptor Inc.! This is Susan!" a gregarious woman chirped, her voice reminiscent of Ms. Frazzle of *Magical Schoolbus* fame. I explained my predicament to her.

"Well, could you give me a brief description of the bird?" Susan asked. I shuffled to my bedroom window and peeked between the window blinds, hoping to catch a glimpse of the bird's body. Nothing. I was only left with the option of imitating the bird's call, but I couldn't bring myself to hooting into my phone.

"Are you sure it's not a mourning dove?" she asked with a serenity that gutted my plea of all of its urgency.

"I couldn't tell you. I don't know much about birds." My response was curt; I so desperately did not want this conversation to turn into a bird species guessing game.

"Do you know anyone that can help me get rid of it?" I was at her mercy.

"Well . . ." she began in a way that already alerted me to the fact that her response would not be palatable—

"If you go with Animal Rescue, you're going to have to catch it yourself, then they would come pick it up."

I heard the loud sound of screeching tires in my head. *Me? Catch a bird?* I scrambled to find the words to end the call. I needed to be polite, though. Susan was, of course, simply a messenger who'd gotten caught in my wild animal crossfire.

"I . . . I don't *do* catching birds." I marveled at the way the words rolled off of my tongue. I'd secretly hoped that the extra heap of sass would advance my cause, that she'd feel the pressure of the "no nonsense" tone in my voice and give me some secret phone number that only granted services to VIP complainers.

Her silence promptly disabused me of this dream.

"Thanks for your help," I ended the call and shrank in momentary defeat. I sought refuge in my bedroom, looking through its window every few minutes. I was determined to verify the identity of what had taken residence in my residence.

What I uncovered: There was no bird inside my air conditioner, but rather under it.

What I confirmed through a quick Google search: The bird that I so badly wanted to be a raptor was in fact a mourning dove.

Ah. A mourning dove. A remixed pigeon, I thought to myself, contemplating the labor of my air conditioner and all of the filth of the city being tirelessly cycled into my living room.

I was perplexed—why did the mourning dove choose to live under *my* air conditioner? Why not the apartment right above or right below mine, both equipped with their own units? The bird's arrival made me nervous. Given my allergies and the harmful pathogens carried by some birds, I really hated the idea of what might invisibly enter my living space. I also just wanted so badly to be by myself. Never had it felt more annoying to be the perfect home for what I did not want to host.

I craved control of my own space because I was well aware of what the opposite of this looked like.

✳

Prior to moving to Cincinnati, I'd spent three years in Indiana, earning an MFA in creative writing and subsequently reimagining my life. While I'd done just fine in my classes during the first year of my program, I hadn't fully transitioned into grad school life or Bloomington, a small, blue-dot-of-a-town in a red, red state. As liberal as Bloomington was, I couldn't help but think about its periphery and borders; I had never seen so many American flags hanging, posted, perched, or adhered to so many surfaces in my life. Patriotism defied gravity. I hadn't been ready for these changes and coped in the best way I'd known how: debauchery.

Somehow in my busy, academically productive schedule, I'd found time to engage in risky romantic encounters, foster toxic friendships, and revel in the cheapness of Midwestern excess, which was markedly more affordable than Californian hedonism. Although I was a broke grad student, I felt very little financial guilt when kicking back shot after shot of Bulleit bourbon, drinking Rhinegeist beer by the pint, and smoking Camel Crushes or American Spirits, depending on my broody artist mood. This is was primarily how I numbed and suppressed the anxieties of grad school and the culture shock of moving to a small town in Indiana. I also gave many of my behaviors a "pass," as they didn't stray from the trope of the lush writer, one of the surest and most welcomed archetypes in grad school. While I felt I was performing what was expected of me as an artist, it became unwieldy, overpowering my capacity to deal.

In the six months that I'd lived in Bloomington, I'd vomited in more public restrooms than I could count and had more blackouts than I could literally remember. I was aching, and had been for a while, but knew no alternative to how I had been living in recent years. I wanted to be done with my blues. My low, breaking, and turning points all came in February 2016, which coincided with the start of Lent. While I thought that I was just "testing out" an alcohol-free life for forty days, it stuck. The start of the journey had been quite tumultuous, anxiety-inducing and miserable. The nectar of sobriety, however, continued to leave an unmatched sweetness that sticks to my spirit.

On certain mornings in Indiana, I would lie still, contemplating the depth of this new calm. I recalled the pain I could no longer feel—there was no more waking up from splitting hangover headaches, neither was there trying, to no avail, to recount the moments from the night before, being frightfully unsure of what I may have said or done a mere few hours before. This stillness felt fresh and sacred. I knew that it was some profound confluence of slowing down and having faith in something bigger than myself that permitted this change.

I was gaining what I would call a miraculous clarity, one that helped me see all that had contributed to a type of dimming of my soul. This was an involved process, this purging of old ways of being. I reflected heavily and often. I was now in the business of questioning everything and everyone as a form of self-preservation. I prayed more and attended church consistently for the first time in my life. I kept away from people and places that might cause me to return to what no longer served me. Being alone enhanced my awareness of my triggers, the weight of my vices, and attuned my ear to the seemingly innocuous lilt of their seductive calls. Solitude was my Polaris. I felt this serenity in my waking hours and in my sleep. It kept the candles that guided my pathway burning. It held up the walls of my living space. There was so much less noise to contend with. Silence actually had a sound; it was my own voice.

So much of my growth occurred in the trusty confines of my apartment, a place in which I felt safe to dream. This was the first time that I created home on my own. This small, sparsely furnished space was my sanctuary and I protected it fiercely. Since experiencing this balance, I could not accept a standard of living of any lesser quality. My tranquility was to be defended at all costs. I hadn't felt this clear-headed, lucid, focused, and deliberate in several years. I was certain I could make no mistakes in my seemingly simple quest for peace.

*

I'm embarrassed to disclose how much of my summer and money I dedicated to dealing with my bird problem. Getting rid of the mourning dove became my passion project. I searched for ways to permanently dissuade the bird from returning to my window. I considered some of the following possibilities:

There was bird glue, which, after squeezing just a few drops in the desired area, would immobilize an unsuspecting bird. In attempts to free itself from the viscous force field beneath its feet, it would violently thrash itself about, to the point of bodily harm. This ensured imminent mortality. The bird glue seemed too cruel an action to take against the mourning dove. I found it odd that this product was on the market, and odder still that the overwhelming amount of customer reviews skewed so positively.

There was the pernicious call of the peregrine falcon, a known and feared enemy of the mourning dove. I was grateful to the avid bird watcher that uploaded falcon footage on YouTube—I was ready to traumatize the mourning dove. I cued up the video, placed my Bluetooth speaker against the window, and blasted the sound for several minutes. While I gave myself what felt like an IMAX experience of a *National Geographic* documentary, the mourning dove couldn't care less—that would have been impossible. I observed its apathy from my bedroom window. While the cacophony bounced against my apartment walls, the mourning dove calmly adjusted itself, as if to rest more comfortably, in preparation for my next stunt.

I'd read that birds were afraid of seeing their own reflections in holograms. The surprise encounter would be so jarring that in the bird's mind, it became the prey that it feared. I bought a prismatic streamer and taped it against my window. As history had been teaching me, this measure too would be ineffectual. The mourning dove would pay me no mind as I armed myself against its presence. It looked like a joke, as if I was decorating for a child's My Little Pony–themed birthday party. While I gave the streamer a week, it had only taken me a few days to know that it wouldn't work.

Aside from the streamer, bird spikes were the only other alternative I was willing to pursue. The image in my Amazon shopping cart was intimidating—the contraption consisted of several rows of long, jutting metal spikes protruding from an adhesive strip to be affixed to the areas trafficked by birds. In spite of how the spikes looked, the reviews assured me that the birds would not be harmed, but instead annoyed enough to not return.

I set up a TaskRabbit appointment to install the spikes around the perimeter of both the window ledge and the air conditioner, rendering it impossible for the mourning dove to return. It was only after the completion of the TaskRabbit worker's service that I realized how much space remained between the air conditioner and the spikes; the mourning dove probably thought that we'd been renovating in anticipation for its next homecoming.

✳

The bird came back. From my bedroom window, I noticed a few twigs under my air conditioner, then a few more, then the creation of what I wanted to believe was an incomplete basket.

*

I avoided turning on the air conditioner for as long as I could, cringing each time I recalled the internet articles that substantiated my very real fear of germs. I read so much on the internet because I had so much time. I had so much time because I had yet to start classes or make any friends in my new town. I had so much time, and had probably gotten too introverted, too inside myself. Idle. I was lonely.

I relied on the relief of fans and open windows until the heat became so unbearable that I could do nothing but cave. The air conditioner revved up for the first time in weeks, but didn't produce a noticeable breeze. Instead, it shot out air the color of skim milk. A foggy exhaust pooled and hovered in the living room.

I set up another TaskRabbit appointment to uninstall my air conditioner. Fortunately, it was still under warranty and could be returned to the store.

*

The TaskRabbit worker removed the bird spikes, then the air conditioner, tilting all of the water from the unit onto the grounds twenty-five feet below my window.

"You want to get rid of it?" he asked as he pointed to what had formed below the unit: a nest which held two small white eggs, only one of which was cracked. Surprisingly, there was no bird in sight.

"Yeah," I responded with an unshakeable malevolence.

The nest, in its lightness, slowly coasted from the ledge until it was no longer visible.

*

As the nest fell, the mother rose.

✻

The mourning dove fluttered its wings frenetically, just quickly enough to maintain a steady bob in my line of vision. With only the closed window between us, it looked at me in my eyes, or somewhere behind them. What it reflected back was the tiny plot of land within me, the scorched earth where only remorse can grow.

✻

The mourning dove stared at me and asked the unanswerable question:
    Why?
    The mourning dove stared at me until it became my hologram and entered me. It disappeared, then sank into my womb.

Forgive me.

It happened quickly.

What wouldn't I kill to keep my home safe?

My good God, I couldn't control the animal in me.

Scenes from July 2013

EMILY HEIDEN

I get the number of a local ob-gyn from a friend and on a Monday morning before work, while sitting on the couch and sipping a ginger ale, I call. They're a few streets away from my Northern Virginia apartment, and I'm hoping maybe they can see me later that day. I fidget as the phone rings, eager to get this process, whatever it is, underway.

"Hello?" a receptionist answers.

"Hi," I say. "I'm calling because . . . well, I think I'm pregnant, and I'd like to see someone to confirm it."

"Okay," she says. "We typically deliver out of Fairfax Hospital—is that okay with you?"

I pause. She's jumping ahead to the end of the pregnancy, and I'm still grappling with the beginning.

"Um," I tell her, shifting my weight on the sofa. "I'm not sure if . . . I'm going to get to delivery."

"Oh." There is a pause. "Well then let me give you a number for another place you can call."

And just like that, thirty seconds into this phone call, I am being turned away. The ob-gyn won't see me. There are other kinds of doctors for women in my position. I want to cry. Her words to me feel as if the world is saying this is not legitimate. You and your pregnancy are not the kind worthy of our time.

Shaking, angry, I punch in the digits of the other number she's given me.

The crepe myrtle's pink blooms shift in a slow breeze on the porch while the phone rings. A prerecorded voice answers.

"You have reached our services. We are not available at this time. Please call back and leave a message on Thursday between 2 and 4 p.m."

Now I am furious. I am not calling back to leave a message on Thursday afternoon. First of all, I'm at work on Thursday at that time, chasing around tiny children, and secondly, it's a Monday morning, and offices are open for business, and I need some help *now*.

After some Googling, I find a clinic in my town that says they will help me, and I make an appointment. They tell me I will have to have an ultrasound, and I don't think to question it. I actually feel relief. Seeing something on a screen means I will know exactly what is happening inside of me. I've envisioned it exhaustively: a moon-white orb floating in a red ocean. A still-flat disc. A strange, neural, sticklike creature, edges just beginning to curve. Picturing this tiny *thing* hidden within my core obsesses me. I can't make up my mind until I know exactly what it looks like. After the ultrasound, I will have the information I need to decide.

I have made a deal with myself: If it looks like a baby, I will keep it. If it doesn't, I won't. This is a tenuous bargain. I don't know whether I will revise it, but on this particular enterprise, I'm flying blind.

So that Saturday, I wake at 8 a.m. and drive across town. The car is quiet, the seats warm with the heat of early July. I pull into a suburban medical office complex, park, and head to the lobby, where I push the button for the elevator and wait.

The place is clean and unremarkable: potted plants, water fountains, people rushing by. The bell dings, and I step inside, scanning the names of offices and doctors on the paneling. But I don't see the name of the clinic I'm looking for. *Where is it?* I think.

I don't yet understand that the fact that I cannot find the name of this clinic listed on the wall is not a mistake. *Have I got the wrong building?* I worry, grabbing out the piece of paper where I've written everything down. *No,* I realize. *This is the right place. It just isn't listed.* A general sense of danger dawns on me. *Why would it be hidden? Is it safe to go here?*

But I go. My paper lists the number of the floor, so I push the proper button and am delivered there.

When I walk into the waiting room, I see a woman in a celery green track jacket working on a grocery list. Her hair is pulled back in a tight ponytail, and she doesn't look at all upset. I wonder for a moment if I've wandered into the wrong office. A slight, beautiful woman sits to my left. She wears a vivid aqua romper, the elastic tight across her breasts and tiny waist. A man is at her side, one hand on her back. They fill out paperwork together. I can't hear their conversation, but their tones seem hushed. Three other women sit behind them.

I sit and wait my turn to go up to the glass window, intensely uncomfortable. The receptionists seem on edge. I imagine that working in a clinic hidden away between floors cannot feel safe or comforting. I try to picture what it would be like to live in a world where clinics like this didn't need to hide. My heart goes out to everyone in this room, myself included. We are all in this shitty boat together. Not that we're really together— we're each quiet, isolated in our private bubbles of experience. We're not making eye contact.

I sit down and wait for the nurse to call my name, riding a wave of nausea. I try to shut off my brain and stare at a fish tank in the corner, where graceful white forms glide silently by. I feel as trapped as they are, but by my female body. I have never understood how vulnerable it makes me until now.

Finally, a woman in a white coat calls my name and walks me down the hall. We go into an office and she invites me to have a seat, then gets right to business.

"First day of last menstrual period?" she asks.

I blink in surprise.

"Uh, June sixth."

"Okay, so that would put you at . . ."

"About four weeks."

"And you've done a home test?"

"Yes," I say, "but that's it so far."

"Those are usually accurate," she shrugs. "Okay, let's go into the other room now."

I stand to follow her. *That's it?* I think.

We head to the room across the hall, which is dimly lit. I lie back in a chair and she tells me to unbutton my jeans, then squirts jelly on my stomach. She pushes a probe into my lower abdomen, and I watch the wand skim over the cold, translucent gel on my skin. All I can think is *I'm having an ultrasound!* I can't keep the silent exclamation point off the end of the statement in my mind. All my life I've wondered about this moment—about the instant I'll first see my baby on a screen. About something this big, this amazing, happening to me.

But I never imagined the moment would be like this. It feels wrong to be excited. I'm fairly sure they perform abortions in this clinic. My mind swirls with anger at myself, and with shame.

The probe pushes harder. It hurts. She furrows her brow at a tiny, boxy, computer-like screen, something that looks straight out of the '80s.

I wait in silence, not wanting to interrupt her. She squints further, then clicks a few buttons. I hold my breath and try not to move.

Finally, I ask, "Can you see anything?"

"Yes," she says.

"Can I see it?" I ask, wondering if I'm crazy to make such a request. I've heard of a lot of people being upset about this issue. They're angry that in some states a woman must have an ultrasound before she can get an abortion, because it can be used as a manipulative tool to guilt someone into continuing a pregnancy they might otherwise have ended. I'm upset about any woman being forced to do something she does not want to do. Yet here I am—in a room with the screen turned away from me, feeling like I'm being denied a pretty critical view.

"Sure," she says, giving a sigh. She pushes a button and prints off a photo. "Here you go."

"Okay. Uhhh . . . where is it?" I reply.

"It's right there," she says, pointing with her pen.

"Oh, okay," I say. "Where?"

"There," she says again, pointing at what looks like a flake of pepper floating in a fuzzy gray sea.

"That's it?" I say. "*That's* my baby?"

"I think so," she says. "I'd put you at four weeks and three days."

"How are you getting this from *that*?" I push, searching for more clear information.

"It has a sac around it."

I look back at the flake.

So does she. We both squint at it one more time.

"You know, let's do a urine test, just to be sure," she says.

✳

In the bathroom, I pee in the cup, then bring her the sample and shift about in a chair while she disappears to test it. I wait until she reemerges a few minutes later. When she appears, I simply look up with the question on my face.

"Yes ma'am," she says in a tone that sounds exhausted, and points to the door where I should exit.

I walk out to the car, trying to process everything, when the baby's father's name lights up the screen of my phone.

Oh my God, I think. I can't deal with him right now. I have no idea what I'll say.

But the fact that he's calling at this moment feels like a sign.

I pick up.

"How are you?" he says.

"Four weeks and three days," I say in my mind.

Out loud, I reply, "I'm good, how are you?" and we talk about the weddings we've both just been to, our jobs, and a movie he wants to see. He asks if I'd like to go with him tomorrow to watch it in Fairfax. I tell him sure. He's a class-mate of mine, and he's so young, so immature. Twenty-four to my twenty-nine. But I'm so wild about him. We've had an off-and-on relationship for months. It's felt like me chasing him for most of that time, but I've been avoiding him since I saw the plus sign on that pregnancy test, so that I can have time to think. And in that space created by my silence, he's finally decided to pursue me. *So this is how to get a guy to chase you, huh?* I think. *Just get accidentally pregnant and go AWOL. Great.*

✳

I go home, sit on my couch, stare outside at the pink flower-ing tree off the porch, and mull over my plan. It did not look like a baby. I could hardly see it.

I tell myself I will make an appointment just in case. I can always cancel it. I have found a clinic in Manhattan that prom-ises to end early pregnancies with very little pain. I've decided that I'll go there if I do choose to end it. But, I remind myself, I don't have to go. I haven't even told Mason yet. Maybe he will want the baby. Part of *me* wants the baby, because it's his.

I think of how beautiful our child would be: a little boy with his father's lustrous hair, thick lashes, perfect nose. I imagine brown eyes and a dewdrop mouth. The term *love child* is a terrible cliché, but that's what this is, I think. For an instant, it feels like nothing short of magic is happening within me.

But reality creeps back in. *I would have to drop out of school,* I think. *I'd have to move home.* I'm not willing to do that. Though I don't really want to, I reach for the phone.

✳

Two nights later we see the film, in which a character describes losing a pregnancy in Paris. I stiffen in my seat beside him in the dark. Surely the cotton sundress I've worn is clinging too tightly about my middle. Can Mason see it? Can he sense it? He must know.

Afterward, in the car, he mentions that it's early, that we could go to a bar. I want to screech *I can't drink,* but instead say, "I have work early tomorrow. I should go home."

Back at my place, he follows me upstairs. He fools around with a song on my iPhone, and I decide this is ridiculous. I just have to tell him. But I'm so nervous. *Isn't there a way around this?* I wonder. Couldn't I just end this on my own, and not let him know? I'm so scared that as soon as I open my mouth, I will lose everything: him and the baby. Both gone from me, just like that.

But I can't keep a secret like this from him. It's too much. I screw up my courage and suck in my breath.

"Would you please come here?" I say. "I have something to tell you."

"That sounded serious."

"It is."

He walks over to the white couch and sits by my side, running a hand through his thick dark hair, as he does when he's nervous. And here it is, the moment to tell him. But all of a sudden, I cannot think of a single way to say it. I can't simply say "I'm pregnant." Those words feel like something from a talk show. I've said them to friends and felt like even *they* were just about to shit themselves. I can't do that to him.

I cast my eyes down at my lap and go silent.

In this silence, I cling to my last moments of hope. I pretend he will pull me to him, cradle me in his arms, look at me with his beautiful brown eyes, whisper we'll be a family. Whether I'm ready for that or not, it's an easier scene to wish for than what I fear: a blank look. Anger. Denial that it's his. A rejection of the baby. Which might feel, I think, like a rejection of me.

When I look back up at him, I see that my silence has said what I couldn't. His mouth is slightly open, in a bit of an *O*. His eyebrows are arched.

"Um," he says, drawing it out and looking at me. He seems nervous and calm at the same time.

"Yeah, uh, well . . . can you guess?" I say, my cheeks flushing with shame.

"Um, *yeah*."

Am I surprised he knew? Was he worried about this happening too?

Then: "It can't be more than . . . five weeks."

And there it is—my answer. He's doing the math, calculating just how early, how undoable it is at this stage. He wants me to get rid of it.

I don't say any of this. I try to appear in control, telling myself I knew this was what he would say. I slowly reply: "You're right; it's not."

"Can't you take the . . . isn't there a pill?"

He knows a surprising amount about this.

"I could. I was going to, but then I read about it and it scared me. One out of a hundred women who take it end up needing surgery to stop the bleeding it causes. I know that's not a huge number, but still."

"Okay," he says.

"Anyway," I say. "I have an appointment on Saturday. At a clinic in Manhattan. My best friend is going to go with me."

He casts his eyes down. I've put the light in them out.

"It's like a bad movie."

"What do you mean?"

His voice drops. "I'm not even going with you."

My heart jumps a tiny bit at this. He wants to be there for me. Or maybe he just knows he probably should be.

But regardless of his statement, I know at this age and stage of his life, even a routine pap smear would freak him out. Never mind a procedure I myself am severely scared to undergo. If he were to come, I would spend my time worrying about how he was doing, and that is obviously something I can't think about at that moment. If anyone is going to come, they need to be my rock.

"It's okay," I tell him. "Kate is going with me."

He doesn't say anything further on the topic, and I let it go. The other thought I'm having is that if he comes with me, I might feel pressured to end it. It is my life, though, that will be the most drastically altered by the decision I make in the clinic room that day. It is not him I should be thinking of. It has to be me.

*

Now I've told him, and as far as he knows, I'm going through with it. One evening later, though, I find myself sitting at my computer screen. It's a dark July night, and I'm opening up a Google page, staring at the blinking cursor in the search field, and searching for pregnancy counseling, then pregnancy help. I don't know what to type. I think back to the counseling I hoped I would get at the clinic where I had the ultrasound. I can't help but feel the guidance I need is out there, that if I just enter the correct words, I will be led to the place that will help me to make up my mind. All I know right now is it's a Tuesday, and there is a tiny beginning of a life in me, and on this coming Saturday if I keep my appointment in New York City, there will not be. That's five days. Five days left to stay this course, get on a train, and undo this thing that—if left in its current state—could undo me.

If I can just get the combination of words right, I know I can find the key to my future, the map to the rest of my life.

My search comes back with clearly Christian sites time after time. Places that talk very openly about Christ and the various ways in which I will suffer forever if I keep that appointment on Saturday.

I move away from them quickly, though they harken to a part of my Roman Catholic upbringing that is difficult to fully push back down. *Will I go to hell if I do this?* I wonder. *Will Mason go to hell?* I do my best to ignore these thoughts, scanning result after result until finally I fall upon a site that feels different from the others.

This one promises no politics, no hype. I click through each of its subcategories and see no mention of Christ. No impending doom. They promise to provide information on abortion, adoption, and pregnancy. I am desperate. I see a number for a hotline and decide to give it a try.

A woman with a very soft voice answers the phone.

"Hello?" she says.

"Hi," I say, quaking in reply.

"How can I help you?" she asks.

"Well, I need to talk to someone about my pregnancy."

"Okay," she says in the same soft tone. "Would you like to come in and see someone in person to talk through that?"

"I can do that?"

"Of course," she says. "What if I schedule you in for tomorrow?"

"Great," I say. "I can come after 5."

The next day, I pass the exit I typically take off 66 West to head home. I drive to a town further south, noting the summer-singed Virginia landscape as I go. Chipotles and Radio Shacks and liquor stores pass by. On a residential street, I find the place.

A little parking lot, several trees. A sign outside advertising pregnancy services. I sit in my car in the parking lot for a moment, smoothing my hair and glancing at my face, which is flushed with the heat of the day and the effort of working with small children. I adjust the sticky collar of my navy polo. I haven't had time to change out of my work clothes, and I wonder what the woman I'm about to meet will think of me. I look like a little prep, someone who should know better than to be showing up at her door.

I enter an empty foyer and look around. There is a buzzer I walk over to and push. A sign tells me to take a seat and wait. I obey.

A moment later, a pretty young brunette wearing a cream-colored cowl-necked sweater and lovely matching heels comes to the door. I notice kind eyes and a heart-shaped mouth as she puts out her hand.

"My name is Lydia," she tells me.

All I can think is that Lydia looks like an angel, and sounds like one too, with that same soft voice I heard on the phone.

She asks me to follow her down the hall, and I oblige. We walk into a nondescript room—slate-gray carpet, blank walls, cherry colored cabinets—and she tells me I should feel free to have a seat on the green couch. I do, dropping my purse at my side.

Lydia sits facing me and crosses her legs, those beautiful cream heels drawing my eyes.

"Would you like a snack?" she asks.

"Ooh," I say. "Well . . . I did just come from work, so I am pretty hungry. What kind?"

She gets up and takes a box from a cabinet, fishes a cookie out of it, and hands it to me.

"Thank you!" I say, tearing into the wrapper.

"No problem," she says. "I work with pregnant women, so I keep cookies on hand at all times." She's grinning, and I laugh back.

And just like that, I'm so relieved, here in this little room with the green couch and the pretty woman and the chewy cookie in my hand.

"So, let's get started, if that's okay," she says.

"Sure," I reply, between bites.

"I have some really dry, boring medical questions to ask you first," she says.

"Okay," I tell her. "Fire away."

"First day of your last menstrual period?" she says.

"June sixth."

"Okay. And you took a home test?"

"Yes, and it was confirmed later by a urine test."

"And you know who the father is?"

"He's a . . . friend," I reply.

"Does he know?"

"Yes."

She stops, seeming to have reached the end of the "dry, boring medical" part, and looks up at me, putting her papers aside.

"Do you have anything else you'd like to tell me, that I didn't ask about?" she says, and with that, I am off, spreading the whole saga before her. How I still can't believe this is happening to me, and how I just can't have a baby right now, but how part of me doesn't want to give it up, and how almost everyone I've talked to says it would ruin my life.

She listens silently as I ramble.

I am embarrassed to lay out my situation, once again feeling myself revealed as the girl who should've been too smart to wind up here, but simultaneously relieved to be with someone trained to help people in my shoes, someone capable of offering the first truly objective feedback I have encountered throughout this entire ordeal.

I finish talking and look up at her, realizing my eyes have been on the floor in front of me. She looks back at me for a minute, as if taking in everything I have just said.

Then she reaches to her left, plucks a tiny piece of paper from the table, and stretches out her arm to hand it to me.

It is a miniature booklet, the size of my palm. The petals of a pink lily stretch across the cover, blooming above a sloping, gentle font that reads "May I Ask You a Question?"

Lydia looks at me and begins to speak in an even softer tone than she used before. "Emily, I'd like to talk with you about something now that is very important to me, for just a couple minutes, if that's okay with you."

"Okay," I say.

"Why don't you turn with me to page 1?"

I open the little booklet up.

Lydia speaks as I read, her voice blending with the words before me on the page to create a confusing effect, momentarily keeping me from processing the text in front of my eyes. I read, without understanding, the question "Has anyone ever taken a Bible and shown you how you can know for sure that you're going to Heaven?"

But then the little black-and-white graphic emblazoned with the words "Holy Bible" jumps out at me from the corner of the page and I want to drop the little booklet at Lydia's beautiful heels and run from the room.

I have been tricked.

Lydia is not an angel, here to help me. She and her front foyer full of chairs and the little bell and the room with the green couch and the cabinets full of chewy cookies and dry, boring medical questions that promise help without politics or hype are a pack of lies.

The lines on the next page confirm these thoughts when they tell me that "the Bible contains both bad news and good news," and that "the bad news is something about [me]" and the "good news is something about God." It tells me we are all sinners, that we have all come short of God's standard of perfection, and that the penalty for sin is death. It goes on to explain that the good news is that Christ died for me, that I can be saved through faith in Christ. It asks me to list four reasons that anything might be keeping me from trusting Christ. Why not pray right now, it says, and tell God that I am trusting his son.

I flip through these pages numbly while Lydia talks, no longer hearing her words at all, too dragged down by the sinking in my mind.

There is no one who will help me to decide.

I am sitting here with a woman who works for an organization that lures desperate women like me into its office with the promise of neutrality and free pregnancy tests, then tells us that if we don't keep our babies, we cannot be with God.

I want to blame Lydia for this moment and explain to her how much I could use someone to sit down with me and simply say, "Okay, let's talk about what would really happen in your life if you had a baby." I want to explain that this approach is the one and only method that might stand a chance of convincing me not to keep my appointment on Saturday.

As I sit here thinking these things, I look at Lydia and see that she believes what she is saying to me with all her heart.

That in her soft words she is pleading with me to see it too, that in her way, she wants to help me and feels this is the only means of doing that.

Because I'm still so mad at myself for getting pregnant in the first place, I put up with what comes next as I sit there on the couch.

We move from the booklet to a larger pamphlet entitled "Before You Decide."

On its cover, a woman with downcast eyes sits on some cement steps and looks like she's thinking a pretty heavy thought. Inside, its pages tell me that I may see this unplanned pregnancy as a major roadblock in my life. They tell me to be encouraged to know that many women in the same situation have found the necessary resources to make positive choices and realize their dreams.

They tell me that abortion is a life-changing event with significant physical, emotional, and spiritual consequences. They tell me most women who struggle with past abortions say they wish they had been told all the facts about abortion.

The pamphlet says I have the right to continue this pregnancy, in spite of pressure from my partner, husband, or parents to make a quick decision.

Its pages go on to describe fetal development in a way I notice does not feel quite right.

It tells me on day one, the baby's features, including sex, hair, and eye color, are determined.

It tells me at week four, the baby's heart is pumping and his or her movement is easily seen on an ultrasound.

It tells me at week six, the baby has fingers and has begun to move, although the mom cannot yet feel his or her movement.

It shows very clear, colored photos of tiny little fingers and large, zoomed-in shots of pink fragile faces with closed eyes and teeny fingernails.

I notice, as I look closer, that near each number—week four, week six, etc.—there is a very subtle, smaller gray font

188 · EMILY HEIDEN

that almost disappears against the page, which reads "four weeks from conception/six weeks from the last menstrual period," or "six weeks from conception/eight weeks from the LMP." I realize these captions are meant to make pregnant women think they are farther along than they actually are. They look nothing like the images from my ultrasound, when the pregnancy was barely visible at four weeks.

I try to tell Lydia about this, shifting in my seat, feeling almost guilty to be arguing with her.

"These pictures don't fit with what I saw last week—" I begin.

"Seventy-nine medical experts are cited in this pamphlet," she says.

"But I've seen—"

"Every image here is medically accurate. You can refer to the back of the pamphlet for more information," she proclaims with such assurance that I stop speaking.

I cast my eyes down. Her words have an effect like doublethink, shifting my knowledge of the truth until I can begin to allow for the possibility that Lydia's statements could somehow be true too.

Then she tells me that although the clinic is closing, she needs five more minutes of my time. She wheels a little TV and VCR into the room and pushes *play*. In the video that comes on, a woman explains that she found out she was pregnant when she hadn't been planning on it, and was very scared, but that the agency in which I was now sitting had given her the resources she needed to keep her child. Story after story like this one follows, woman after woman expressing gratitude for her children.

This is followed by people claiming to be doctors describing what they say are the dangers of various abortion procedures: scarring, rupturing uteri, infertility, bleeding out on the table. If you have this procedure, they imply, you are going to lose your ability to have babies, or be scarred physically, emotionally, or spiritually. Or die.

Afterwards, I am shaking. I tell Lydia a lot of those things are not true.

"The wording in that video is misleading," I say. "And it's not really even a baby at most of the stages they're talking about. In these early weeks—in the one I'm in now—it's just a ball of cells."

Lydia looks back at me. "I think we both know, Emily, that it's more than just a ball of cells."

I want to hate her in this moment. But all I can do is look back at her big brown eyes, knowing I wouldn't be here, trying to dissect the entire phenomenon on her green couch, if I truly believed what I've just told her, that what's inside of me is anything other than the beginning of a whole, entire possible life. A dark-haired boy who looks like his beautiful father. A girl who's blue-eyed and fair-skinned like me.

"I have to go," I say, and Lydia presses a card into my hand. "Remember we're here for you," she tells me as I walk out of the room. I hold back my tears until I get to the car. The following day, Lydia calls. "I just want to follow up, Emily," she says in a voicemail, and invites me to speak further with her. She calls the next day, too. She calls Sunday, on my train ride back from Manhattan. I watch her number light up the screen. Finally, I pick up, and in a voice that betrays both emptiness and relief, I tell her that I did decide.

Can You Tell Me What You Saw?

LEE MARTIN

It starts with a glimpse—the bare soles of my mother's feet poking out from the hem of her cotton nightgown as she kneels beside her bed. I've come upon her by accident, and when I do, I immediately retreat to the living room and stand there, ashamed, until I hear the bedsprings creak, and I know my aged mother has placed her hands on the mattress to push herself up from her knees. I feel guilty, not so much because I've found her at what must be a private nightly ritual but more because I imagine she's praying for me, her only child, who's turned away from the church.

I've come to tell her I'm sorry for being snappish earlier in the evening. Since my father's death a few years prior, she's lived alone in this house, and I'm sorry I don't live closer. I'm sorry I have a life in Ohio while she lives out the rest of hers alone in Illinois. I'm sorry I lost my temper with her because her dog—a Chihuahua named Cuddles—isn't house-trained and keeps making messes on the carpet.

"You can't let this keep happening," I said, and my ever-gracious mother never raised her voice. She patiently cleaned the carpet.

"Well," she said, drawing out the word. "Now," she said. She was speaking just above a whisper, as if to say . . . well . . . as if to say there wasn't anything else to say.

What did I know of the lonely days of her widowhood? A young couple from her church had given her the dog for company. How could I presume to question the adjustments she must have made—the dog being one of them—to make up for my father's absence?

"I've taken care of someone all my life," she said when she first saw him in his casket. It was before the visiting hours began. She pressed a handkerchief to her mouth and choked out a sob. "What am I supposed to do now?"

*

My father died on a hot day near the end of July. It was nearly evening, around five o'clock, when he said he was going to mow the back yard. My mother was cooking their supper.

"It's nearly done," she told him. "Why don't you wait?"

Our house had no air conditioning. I can imagine the heat of the kitchen, the flames of the gas burners on my mother's stove, the box fan circulating the warm air, ruffling the pages of the First National Bank calendar on the wall by the tele-phone. I smell the hot grease, the fried hamburger. I watch the sweat pool in the hollow of my mother's throat between her collarbones. I hear the tap of her spatula against the rim of the frying pan.

This was three years after my father's heart attack. He'd done the rehab and dropped a lot of weight. He'd walked this town, a cane with him to fight off stray dogs. He'd pedaled a stationary bike with a fierceness that left him sweat-soaked.

He'd continued to farm our eighty acres ten miles south of town.

He'd known manual labor all his life. He had a lawn to mow, and a few minutes before supper to make some headway. *Day's a wastin'*, he used to tell me when I dragged my feet in the morning because I didn't want to work on our farm. *Mister, shake a leg.*

I wasn't there when he walked out the back door. "Just call me," he told my mother, "when it's time to eat."

In 1955, when I was born, we lived in a 1920s-era farmhouse in Lukin Township. This was in southeastern Illinois, three hours due east of St. Louis, nearly as far as you could go before crossing the Wabash River into Indiana. My parents married in 1951 when my father was thirty-eight and my mother was forty-one. Four years later, I came along, a surprise baby born to my parents who were in the middle of their surprising lives. They'd found love later than most. My mother must have thought she'd be a spinster schoolteacher all her life. My father surely assumed he'd go on caring for his nearly-blind mother in that farmhouse that had passed from my great-grandparents, to my grandparents, and then to my father. I was my parents' only child, the last of the Martin line.

"Don't get married until you're over thirty," my father told me when I was eighteen and then nineteen, but I didn't take his advice.

I'm not sure why, but I was in a hurry to find a girl and jump the broom. Maybe my impatience had something to do with the fear I had when I was growing up that my parents would die before I could marry, and then there I'd be, alone. Maybe it was collateral damage, the unavoidable wound that came from the fact that I came to my parents so late in their lives. Maybe I grew up always afraid that the people I loved would leave me.

"You just cried and cried," my aunt told me long after the November day in 1956 when my father, trying to clear the corn that was clogging up his picker's shucking box, got first one hand and then the other trapped between the spinning rollers, and a surgeon amputated those hands, leaving my father to wear prostheses—his hooks—the rest of his life. "I'd bring you to the hospital waiting room each day at noon, and Beulah (my mother) would come down to hold you, but you wouldn't go to her. You just clung to my neck, and you wouldn't let go."

Imagine being that young—maybe the afternoon of my father's accident, I was sitting on our farmhouse's hard linoleum floor, fascinated by the dust motes dancing about in a ray of sunlight streaming through the window, or perhaps I was sleeping beneath my quilt, sleeping a deep, peaceful sleep— and being snatched up and spirited away, your father nowhere to be seen, your mother handing you over to your aunt and hurrying away herself. You don't know the words *hospital,* or *snapping rollers,* or *amputation.* You only know the unsettling feeling of trouble, of separation, or abandonment. No matter how much someone loved you, wouldn't you spend your life searching for something solid to anchor you to this earth, something you feel you can trust?

❋

After my father died, my mother relied on others for her transportation. She'd had a driver's license when she was younger, and I remember a two-toned Chevy—blue and white—that she drove to the grade school where she taught, but then she lost that position when the school board refused to renew her contract because there was the impression that she had trouble disciplining her students. That impression may have been accurate because my mother was a kind person, a little timid, who always believed in the best parts of people. It would have been very easy for students to have taken advantage of her soft heart. I was stunned, though, to hear a story after she was dead that once she'd become so frustrated with the poor behavior of one boy that she brought a rope to school and tied him to his desk. If that's a true story, I feel confident that it hurt my mother to have to do that. If the world could be the world she preferred, all of us would be compassionate, polite, and full of love. I can only recall a handful of times when she came close to saying a critical word about someone.

Once, when I was complaining about the untidy habits of my then-wife and how hard it was to live in a house of clutter, my mother said, "I don't believe housekeeping holds much interest for her."

Another time, my mother faced the truth of a man who went to her church, a man who wasn't, as we said back then, "work brittle," a man who moved from job to job and probably drank too much. My mother had sympathy for him and whatever demons he had because her father had gone through a similar time—arrests for public drunkenness, a farm lost, and a skip northward looking for work—but she was mainly concerned about his wife. "That poor man," my mother said. "Something's haunting him." She was quiet for a moment, and then she added, "You know, Helen could have done so much better than him."

The point is my mother rarely criticized, and when she did, it was clear that it cost her something, some part of her belief in goodness.

When we moved to a suburb of Chicago—my mother had found a teaching position there—she let her driver's license expire. When we moved back downstate six years later, she had no desire to start driving again. My father was her chauffeur.

Perhaps she gave little thought to what she'd do once he was gone.

I wasn't there to witness the accommodations she had to make in her widowhood, but they're vivid and regrettable in my imagination, because two weeks after my father's death, I moved to Fayetteville, Arkansas, to go to graduate school. I almost didn't go. How could I leave my newly widowed mother alone in that house? She'd have to walk uptown and carry her groceries home, or else wait until a friend with a car offered to drive her. She'd have to ask for rides to her church, which was twelve miles away. My mother, who always hated to bother other people, would now have to rely on their kindness, would have to become what she never wanted to be, a burden to someone else.

The night of my father's visitation, we came back to the house from the funeral home and sat around the chrome-edged dinette set where once upon a time I'd gathered with my mother and my father, and I told my mother I didn't think I should go to Arkansas.

She knew it was my dream to be a writer. I'd tried once to get into the MFA program at Arkansas and hadn't been admitted. She knew the acceptance of my second application meant the world to me. I wanted to write, and I wanted to teach. I wanted to live in the world of books, a world my mother made possible for me because it was a world that mattered to her, too. When I was a child, she read to me from my Little Golden Books. A few years later, she enrolled me in a children's classics book club. She was with me the first time I stepped into a library. She'd shown me that the world was larger and more varied than our small town. Now I had a chance to leave it, but my father was dead, and I couldn't face the thought of my mother alone with her grief.

"I can't leave you here," I said that night at our dinette set.

She sat across from me, her face drawn with sadness and fatigue. We weren't the kind of family who showed our affection. We didn't hug or kiss or pat one another on the arm. We rarely said "I love you." Instead, we expressed our love with our actions—the way my father patiently drove my mother where she needed to go, the way he insisted she buy new dresses even when she said she didn't need them, the way my father ferociously stood up for me when he thought I'd been wronged, the way I so desperately wanted to please him.

My mother simply said, "You father would want you to go."

It was true. I knew it right away. My father, who'd overcome so much with his determination and spirit, was nothing if not a fighter. Despite the troubles between us—and there'd been many—he wanted me to have what I wanted.

"He's all grown up," he'd said to a high school friend of his a few weeks before he died. "I guess I can rest now."

So I went to Arkansas, and all the while I was there, I saw images in my mind that I'd rather not have seen—my mother sitting at the table with her supper each evening while the dark of autumn and then winter came on earlier and earlier; my mother, her cheeks caved in without her dentures, her hair unpinned and braided, reaching for the bedside lamp as she put another day behind her; my mother, looking out the window, watching the cars go by on the street, the schoolkids skipping by on the sidewalk. She described their bright voices to me in a letter. *Mercy,* she wrote. *How it made me wish I was teaching again.*

Then there were the stories people told me, stories that put scenes in my head that filled me with guilt.

My mother, walking home from uptown, saw a kid's stuffed bear leaning against the trunk of a tree. A woman who worked at the bank saw my mother pick up the bear and walk away with it.

"I thought, my goodness," the woman said, "that's not something Beulah would do."

Indeed it wasn't, nor would she, if she hadn't been so lonely, let a family of kids who lived in a house trailer one street over, into her house.

"They're stealing from her," the same woman at the bank told me. "They come in with blank checks she's signed. The oldest girl makes them out to herself and fills in the amount."

"And the bank cashes them?" I said.

"We called your mother, and she told us to go ahead."

So there was that to see as well: my mother signing a check and handing it over to this girl.

"Your mother goes away and leaves those kids in the house," a neighbor told me. "It's like they've moved in and made themselves at home."

＊

My father's supper was on the table that hot day in July. My mother was about to turn toward the door, about to go out into the back yard and call him in.

Then she heard the mower roar and saw him lying on the grass.

He was already gone, a neighbor told me later. Myocardial infarction, the death certificate would read. A heart seized. The blood flow stopped. A weight in the chest before the nothingness came.

I wasn't there to see it happen. When the neighbor called to tell me they'd taken my father to the hospital, I said, "I should call there, then, right? The hospital?"

The neighbor, a kind and gentle retired teacher—he'd been in his own yard and he'd seen my father fall and he'd come to start CPR—said, "You should come. You should come right now."

That evening is now thirty-six years in the past. I had no idea, then, what lay ahead. I didn't know the trouble my first wife and I would have. I couldn't have foreseen the anguish of divorce or the miracle of reconnecting with a girl I loved when she was in high school and I was a freshman in college, and being married to her now and living with our little orange cat in such bliss. We move along, not quite feeling the current. Time. It just goes. What's the old joke about the snail who was mugged by a gang of turtles?

"It was horrible," the snail told the police.

An officer said, "Can you identify them? Can you tell me what you saw?"

"No," the anguished snail said. "It happened so fast."

I'm sixty-three years old now, six years younger than my father was when he died and left my mother to her widowhood.

The last thing I said to my father was, "Don't work too hard."

He told me he wouldn't.

It was something men said to one another in the agricultural Midwest, nonchalant words of parting, at the least. At best, an unemotional way of expressing affection.

Don't work too hard. I care about you.

Who knew it would be the last thing I'd say to my father? Who knew it would be the last time I saw him alive?

For a long time after his death, I saw him everywhere. At my mother's house, whenever I got up at night and passed through the family room on my way to the bathroom, I swore I saw him sitting in his chair. In dreams, I came upon him while walking down a sidewalk in a town I didn't know. *You're supposed to be dead,* I'd say to him in the dream. Just like that he'd crumple to the ground as if he were a marionette whose strings had been cut.

I still see the moment of his death even though I try my best not to imagine it. The sweat running from beneath his cap, pooling in his eyes, gathering in the hollow of his throat; the mower's handle gripped between the pincers of his hooks, the pincers he must have opened when he felt his heart explode. I can't stop myself from imagining that moment, nor can I erase the image of his lifeless body. Sometimes I see it face down, his cap askew, and sometimes I imagine he fell backward and lay on the grass, eyes open, but seeing nothing of the sky above him.

If only I'd been there to mow that yard. If only I hadn't been the absent son.

＊

All my life, I've tried to come home. Since the day of my father's corn-picker accident, when I was whisked away to my aunt and uncle's, I've longed for the steadfast, reluctant to admit what I've surely known all along: Nothing stays.

What does it mean to call a place home? To call people family? To rest secure without fear of abandonment? What does it mean to be truly content and happy?

I'm closer now to knowing the answers, than, perhaps, I've ever been. I wake each morning in a home I love with a woman I love and a little orange cat who rubs against my legs when I'm putting her food in a bowl and later comes to my study and gets on my lap, purring and kneading while I write. I live without anger and drama. I live with a woman I trust, a woman I first loved when I was too young to know what to do with that love. Our little orange cat, Stella, came home with us from the humane society a year ago, and that first night, she curled up on Cathy's chest and has trusted us ever since. Right now, as I type this, she sleeps in her cat tree by a window where the sun warms her. I have to believe she knows we're hers just as we know she's ours. We've promised one another, the three of us, to live in peace and love for however long the journey may last.

My mother believed in God's love. Through all the challenges her life gave her—my father's accident, motherhood in midlife, my teenage rebellion, my father's death, my absence—her faith never wavered. She was never evangelical. Her faith was a private matter. The sight of her on her knees beside her bed, her hands pressed together in prayer, offered the most intimate portrait imaginable. To come upon her there, her gray hair hanging down her back in a braid, the soles of her feet bare beneath the hem of her gown, was a gift, and yet I wish I'd never seen her that night. Shame over my own separation from the church—my own life that had been full of mistakes; my own guilt for not being the son she wished I could be—wouldn't allow me to appreciate the sight of my mother in prayer.

I should have fallen down on my knees beside her. If I close my eyes, I can see the two of us in the lamplight, our heads bowed. When I was a boy, she taught me how to pray. *Now I lay me down to sleep. I pray the Lord my soul to keep.* In the night, when I woke, afraid of the dark, I called for her, and she always came. She sat on the edge of the bed until I fell back asleep. In my turbulent teenage years, when I had trouble sleeping, she told me to count my blessings. I remembered the hymn we sang in church:

> Count your blessings;
> Name them one by one.
> Count your blessings;
> See what God hath done.

Why couldn't I trust and believe the way she did? Why couldn't I give her this one thing she wished—an upright, Christian son—in return for all the sacrifices she'd made and all the gifts she'd given me? Why couldn't I have knelt beside her that night and asked for forgiveness?

The image flutters behind my eyelids for a moment and then it's gone, and what I see instead of my mother and I praying is the scratched and faded hardwood floor after I'd sold all of my mother's belongings at auction, and then the house itself, all signs of the life we once lived there gone for good.

"I'm sorry," I told my mother that night after she'd finished her prayer. "I'm sorry I was angry with you about the dog." I searched for all the words I wanted to say. "I really wasn't angry with you," I said. "It was the dog, and it was the people who gave it to you, and it was the mess it made, and . . ."

"I know," she said in her kind voice that seemed a bit weary now. "Go to sleep," she told me, and it was as if I were a boy again. "Things will seem brighter in the morning," she said. "They always do."

One day in spring, Cathy and I went back to the farm where once upon a time I lived with my parents. The lane was full of foxtail and milkweed and cocklebur. We walked to the dip where a rivulet ran through an old culvert and then made the final rise to the farmyard. It, too, was weed-choked, but I found a bit of concrete that marked the walkway that led up to where the side door had once opened onto the enclosed wash porch A tall maple tree had come crashing down on the house during a storm, leaving a pile of debris where that wash porch had been. I made my way around the back of the house, and I got close enough to peer through the debris. I saw the kitchen cabinets still intact, the refrigerator and the gas stove. Everything else was gone. The drop-leaf table where we ate our meals, the two pie safes, the library table where my mother, in an old photograph I've saved, sat to feed me when I was a baby. She holds me on her lap and puts a spoon to my lips. I grab onto the handle. Am I saying, I can do it myself? Or am I saying, Please, don't ever leave me?

I wasn't with my mother when she died. She died with her brothers and sister around her in the nursing home. I was living six hours away in Memphis at the time, wanting to, but trying not to, imagine the scene.

This is the last thing I wish I could keep myself from seeing. My mother in her bed, her eyes closed, her cheeks sunken without her dentures, her eye blackened and her face bruised from a recent fall, her breaths coming farther and farther apart, her lungs struggling to work. Everything is shutting down. And then the death rattle, saliva gathering in her throat and bronchial tubes. The skin on her hands is mottled with purple blotches. Her lips have a bluish tinge. My aunt is holding her hand. My uncles are telling her it's all right. She doesn't have to fight. She can go.

And so she does. She slips away, and I spend years and years holding onto the last items that she owned: a black pocketbook with a gold clasp, a Royal gift stamp kept in a wallet, an embroidered handkerchief from the Wisconsin Dells, her last Bible. It hurts me to see them, but how can I look away?

That day with Cathy at the ruined farmhouse, I looked into the living room where an old couch sat sunken and worn, and the fuel oil stove was rusted. It was enough to bring back the life my parents and I had lived there. I could see the little boy I was curled up on that couch, or sitting on the linoleum floor with my Lincoln Logs, or at that stove when my mother curled a cone from newspaper, lit it with a match, and swirled it around the stove's drum. It was warm near the heat. Some days I drifted off to sleep on that couch while the wind howled outside and the snow came down, and when I woke, it was dark, and my mother was in the kitchen and she, hearing me stir, told me to wake up, sleepyhead, it's time for supper. So I rose and went to her voice, and we sat with my father at our table, and we were a family.

I wish I could tell my mother that Cathy and I took three things from the house. Part of a door frame that Cathy turned into a shelf that hangs in our house and holds old photos of my parents and me along with artifacts from my family: my baby rattle, my mother's school bell, the lid to a cream pitcher, an old medicine bottle—the things the living leave behind.

We took that length of door frame, and Cathy cleaned and stained it. We also took a piece of clapboard siding. Cathy printed our last name on it along with the plat description of the farm—its section and range and township. Then she drew an outline of that township and she marked the creek that ran through our land in blue, and with a red dot, she marked the location of this house, the one that exists now only in my memory. This sign now hangs in our hallway. I give thanks for the company of a woman who would take such selfless care to honor and preserve. I wish my mother could see, at the end of the crooked road I traveled, the happiness and love I've found.

The third thing that Cathy and I took was a two-board section of the hardwood floor—the floor my parents had covered with linoleum. On it, Cathy painted this verse from the Book of Ruth: "for whither thou goest, I will go; and where thou lodgest, I will lodge."

This sign hangs above our bed in this house of loyalty and faith and love.

The night I left my mother for Arkansas, intending to drive through the darkness to St. Louis and then down into the Ozarks, I told her good-bye.

"Be careful," she said.

I was already close to tears. Something was ending—I knew that—and something exciting was about to begin. In many ways, I was still the shy boy who'd once clung to my mother's skirts, the only child, afraid to show my face to the world, but I was also a fatherless son now, ready to make my own way.

"Mom," I said.

We were standing on the porch in the glow of the dining room light coming through the screen door. My mother's back was stooped as if all the years she'd spent with my father were pressing down on her, both his presence and now his absence. Or as if the pain I'd helped cause was pulling her toward the ground. Still she managed a shy grin—always that sweet, shy grin, the look of a woman who had faith that everything would be all right. I wanted to say so much more to her. I wanted to thank her for the love she'd given me, for all the times she'd read to me when I was young, for inviting me to know the world through language and story, for all her faith in me even when I didn't deserve it, for letting me go.

"Let me know that you get there all right," she said.

"I will," I told her, and then I got in the car and pulled out onto the street.

She was still standing on the porch waving at me. I had miles and miles to go, and years and years to live. Although I didn't know it then—could only hope and dream—there would be books for me to write, stories for me to tell, countless students to teach. All I knew that night was that I would have a chance. My father's fire and my mother's encouragement were giving it to me. All the way up the street, I kept glancing in my rearview mirror. She was still there, watching my taillights as I drove away from her.

How could she have known, all those years ago when she read to me, when she enrolled me in that children's book club, when she took me to a library that eventually—it must have seemed like it happened in a blink of an eye—this day would come?

At the end of our block, I turned left. There was nothing now but the empty streets of the town, the lights on in storefronts on the main street, and then the businesses dwindling as I made my way to the highway, the road that would take me out of town, to the flat prairie land where out across the fields pole lights would be on in barnyards, to the steady click of my tires over the seams in the road, each mile taking me closer, and still closer, to where my mother wanted me to be.

If I close my eyes, I can still see her on that porch in the dim light, her hand raised as if to bless me, as if to say, *Go on. Go. Go have the life I gave you.*

Muse of Brooklyn

I Would Never Study but in My Dreams

> Were my memory as faithful as my reason is then fruitful,
> I would never study but in my dreams, and this time also
> would I choose for my devotions; but our grosser memories
> have then so little hold of our abstracted understandings,
> that they forge the story, and can only relate to our awaked
> souls a confused and broken tale of that which hath passed.
>
> —Thomas Browne, *Religio Medici*

My mother on the floor, eye half-opened, the deadest thing. No thou there.

My father in his casket, half-smile on his face. A stupid smile he never would have allowed.

A woman I accidentally saw in the funeral parlor (don't you love the recherché, *"parlor," like we're about to have tea and sugar cookies and talk about the perfect world with its inordinate heat) where I was attending the funeral of my English department chair who had died on Sunday after feeling queasy on Friday. This woman, propped up in her coffin (coffin, casket, no way to sugar-coat those boxes of cookies), had an enormously deformed head that visits me in nightmares.*

207

*

Although all of these *miserables* exceeded what I wished not to see, none exceeds my accumulated desire to not keep seeing what delights and thrills me, what *frissons* me without my quite understanding, in the moment, why. My mother, dead for almost forty years, lives in my dreams, has *always* been alive in my dreams. I have never remembered a dream in which my mother registered as dead. So I dream her alive and then wake to her death, time after time, reenacting grief, having to pay, it seems for some undigested slice of mourning. I'm a Rube Goldbergian, Frankensteinian, Freudian self-punishment machine: self-administering a system of delight, creating resurrection, and tying a bow around it all with the guilt of killing what I revive.

I wish, I wish, I would not have my wish fulfillment fulfilled. I am awash in this wish, and it has saddened me for decades.

It's strange to wish for a desire to be rid of what one has, even if the possession is intermittent. *Possession* isn't quite right, of course—we say we "have" memories, as though they're on the shelves, in our bags, our pockets. We have met the memory, and they are us. And the memory of dreams, no different as memories, are no more or less material than the memory of moments. When we're autopsied, there isn't a tiny blue fluid of "real narrative" unguent, and a smaller few drops of paisley dream liquid that leaks onto the coroner's tools. But, perhaps sometime in the future they'll find a little dream lockbox, deep in one of the cortices, or on some street corner in New Jersey, and this entire paragraph will be just so recherché. Scholars of my work will have to mark it, perhaps here, with an asterisk.

The memory of all of the dreams I've had of my mother alive for the past forty years haunt me, and when the dreams were more frequent—they've gradually diminished over the decades to, maybe, two or three a year—I would dread going to sleep at night because of the delight and despair that would accompany these images, these emotional *trompe l'oeils.*

Here's one dream I remember: I am talking to my brother and I see an airplane taking off at an odd angle. I sensed this was not a good thing, that the plane was struggling. (I'm a post-Freudian Freudian, so have fun with all of the suggestive language.) The plane dipped and slipped and headed towards where my brother and I stood. A crowd around us, newly aware of the danger, scattered. I kept a kind of surreal equipoise. But I moved slowly from the spot as the plane crashed, crash-landed really, and skidded, a couple hundred yards away from me. Considering my relative nonchalance, you'd think my whole life had been a disaster. But my brother had disappeared, and I was overwhelmed with the need to locate him and my mother, who apparently, in the gracefully skewed absurdity of dream narratives, was "somewhere nearby." I found my brother quickly and we headed for a series of underground tunnels near the site of the plane's impact, since the dream, since I (the urge to see dreams as separate entities, as amorphous creatures filled with our psychic energy but somehow independent, has its own overdetermined motivations— we say, "The dream then turned, the dream suggested . . ." as though we were part of the dream, and not the dream, of us) clearly had been turned into the Orpheus to my mother's Eurydice. I needed to descend to save her, and I did, down stairs that were part ancient cave and simply abandoned from some modern building. I don't remember entering, just descending. And in my memory I'm calm, though men and women are rushing past, either escaping from a catastrophe or too close to it, aware of something terrible or part of it. I met my brother at some point, and he was walking up (how did that happen?—everything that rises must converge in dreams) and he said to me that it was okay, she was okay.

So I did not find my mother in the chaos. But when I turned again and walked up the stairs and emerged, I noticed there was a cornfield near where the plane had crashed. Her car was there and I thought, as a non sequitur, *more mothers die in plane crashes than in their cars.* My mother was alive, as usual, in my dreams. I only had to go to that house.

I was full of disquiet.

I never got to the house—I woke up. I always wake up before anything can disturb my mother's livelihood. *Livelihood,* a word we use for work, is too good a word to not try and use in other ways: like the shaded or camouflaged nature of life that dead can acquire in dreams. Their *livelihood,* which we donate to them so we can play with them on the shaky stage we create to not let them go completely, because, you know, we can't, we just can't.

Instead, I woke up. Woke up, got out of bed, dragged the dreams across my head. I'm sure you've experienced the yearning, upon waking, to have the dream continue. It need not even necessarily be a dream whose venue you're enamored of. It's that feeling—part narrative, part geographical—of *I was just so there in that strange and intense place and now I'm just back here, in the familiar dark.* It's a feeling of:

being wrenched
being violently transported
having lost something
having to adapt to a different self, a different ontologi-
    cal state
loss, pure loss
such disconcert that you can lose all sense of where
    you are, the details of time and
    place

This is what happened with that dream, and what has frequently happened in dreams I have had where my mother returns to my consciousness. I remember to breathe, and having no pearls to clutch, clutch at the impressions of dark rooms turning to gray and giving me reminders of who and where I am. David. Home. Son upstairs asleep. Mother still dead.

All right: Clearly mourning has not become me enough, at least subconsciously, so that I can let my mother go. I'm reminded of the deep grief in the James Wright "Jenny poems," especially "To the Muse," poems that I was reading over and over before and after my mother died in 1980, when I was trying to be a poet. Now that I look back on the poem, which is also like a dream, a dream of resisting the fact of a beloved's death, I wonder if I fell in love with the poem when my mother was dying as a kind of preemptive foreknowledge. I see, too, that James Wright died the same year as my mother, which makes this whole enterprise a bit hallucinatory, as though I were still twenty-three and had been staring too long at a cracked crystal ball.

In the poem, Wright speaks in the present to his dead inamorata, adjusting his rhetoric, first telling her, and himself, that he wouldn't lie to her about the pain she has ahead, only to self-correct and say, "I would lie to you / If I could." He would lie to himself if he could, imagining an Orphic scenario where he leads her, Jenny, back to life, "after dark." After waking himself to the false present, which is to say the remembered past in which she is being treated again for her cancer, as was, unbearably, my mother, he finds that neither memory of her living, since it carries images of her living with pain, nor pulling the nose of the plane up into the present, away from the "black sand" where she *lies, lies* being the writer's word that shows how she is his muse, "muse of black sand," is bearable. The poem with a wild gesture of suicidal remorse: Since the poet hasn't made the world, "this scurvy and disastrous place," and cannot bear his grief, or turn Jenny to Eurydice, he asks his muse to

Come up to me, love
Out of the river, or I will
Go down to you.

Sometimes death kills our ability to grieve, at least to grieve in a way that offers some relief. I could, in my own case, suggest that my own dream-valediction forbidding mourning substituted denial instead. A mechanism. A process. An airplane skids, and, like James Wright, I head down, looking for the dead woman, to make sure she's all right. In my case, through these decades, it's been muse of Brooklyn, appearing most frequently through the windows of a row house, or turning a corner of that old borough carrying a shopping bag and catching a glimpse of me, glad to see me safe. I notice her concern, and her relief. And this, in turn, relieves me.

Contributors

MARY CAPPELLO's six books include a detour (on awkwardness), a breast cancer anti-chronicle, a lyric biography, and a mood fantasia, *Life Breaks In*. Cappello is a former Guggenheim and Berlin Prize Fellow, a recipient of the Dorothea-Lange/Paul Taylor Prize, and a professor of English and creative writing at the University of Rhode Island. Her two new books-in-progress focus on dormancy—its various meanings, shades, disciplinary nooks, and unexpected locales—and the forms that intimacy takes between strangers.

PAUL CRENSHAW is the author of the essay collections *This One Will Hurt You*, published by The Ohio State University Press, and *This We'll Defend*, from the University of North Carolina Press. Other work has appeared in *Best American Essays*, *Best American Nonrequired Reading*, The Pushcart Prize, *Oxford American*, *Glimmer Train*, *Tin House*, *North American Review*, and *Brevity*, among others.

LINA MARÍA FERREIRA CABEZA-VANEGAS was born in Bogota, Colombia, and is the author of *Drown Sever Sing*. Her ode to cannibalism can be found in the collection titled *After Montaigne: Contemporary Essayists Cover the Essays*. She is a graduate of the University of Iowa's creative nonfiction and literary translation programs, and her work has been featured in *Arts and Letters, The Chicago Review,* and *Fourth Genre,* among others. Her book, *Don't Come Back,* is published by Mad Creek Books, an imprint of The Ohio State University Press (January 2017). Ferreira Cabeza-Vanegas is a recipient of the 2016 Rona Jaffe Foundation Writer's Award.

EMILY HEIDEN's work has appeared in *The Washington Post, Literary Hub, Electric Literature, Brevity Magazine, Colorado Review, Juked Magazine, The Hartford Courant,* and *The Seattle Times.* She has an essay forthcoming in the anthology *Fast Women, Flash Fiction,* to be published by Woodhall Press. A PhD student in creative writing and literature at the University of Cincinnati, she holds an MFA in nonfiction from George Mason University and an MAT in teaching from University of Iowa.

SONYA HUBER is the author of five books, including the award-winning essay collection on chronic pain, *Pain Woman Takes Your Keys and Other Essays from a Nervous System.* Her other books include *Opa Nobody* and *Cover Me: A Health Insurance Memoir.* Her work has appeared in the *New York Times, Brevity, Creative Nonfiction,* and other outlets. She teaches at Fairfield University and in the Fairfield low-residency MFA program.

KRISTEN IVERSEN's books include *Full Body Burden, Molly Brown: Unraveling the Myth, Shadow Boxing, Doom with a View,* and a forthcoming literary biography of Nikola Tesla. Her work has appeared in the *New York Times, American Scholar, The Nation,* and many others, and fellowships include the Ohio Arts Council, San Jose Literary Arts Council, Colorado Art Ranch, and the Taft Foundation. Iversen teaches at the University of Cincinnati and is literary nonfiction editor of the *Cincinnati Review.* She is currently a Fulbright Scholar at the University of Bergen.

YALIE KAMARA is a Sierra Leonean American writer and a native of Oakland, California. She's the author of *A Brief Biography of My Name,* which was included in *New-Generation African Poets: A Chapbook Box Set* (Tano) and *When the Living Sing.* She earned an MFA in poetry from Indiana University, Bloomington, and is currently a doctoral student in English literature and creative writing at the University of Cincinnati. For more, visit https://www.yaylala.com.

DAVID LAZAR's books include *Celeste Holm Syndrome* (Nebraska), *I'll Be Your Mirror: Essays and Aphorisms* (Nebraska), *Who's Afraid of Helen of Troy* (Etruscan Press), *After Montaigne* (Georgia), *Occasional Desire: Essays* (Nebraska), *The Body of Brooklyn* (Iowa), and *Truth in Nonfiction* (Iowa). He is founding editor of *Hotel Amerika,* and series editor, with Patrick Madden, of *21st Century Essays,* at The Ohio State University Press. He was a Guggenheim Fellow in Nonfiction for 2015–16.

PATRICK MADDEN is the author of three essay collections, *Disparates* (2020), *Sublime Physick* (2016), and *Quotidiana* (2010), and coeditor of *After Montaigne* (2015). He teaches at Brigham Young University and Vermont College of Fine Arts; with Joey Franklin, he edits the journal *Fourth Genre*; with David Lazar, he edits the *21st Century Essays* series at The Ohio State University Press; and he curates the online essay resource http://www.quotidiana.org.

LEE MARTIN is the author of five novels, including *The Bright Forever,* a finalist for the 2006 Pulitzer Prize in Fiction, and of three memoirs, two short story collections, and a craft book, *Telling Stories.* He is the winner of the Mary McCarthy Prize in Short Fiction and fellowships from the National Endowment for the Arts and the Ohio Arts Council. He teaches in the MFA program at The Ohio State University.

ALYCE MILLER is the award-winning author of five books and more than 250 stories, essays, poems, articles, and book chapters. An ex-Californian, she currently lives in the DC metro area.

AMELIA MARÍA DE LA LUZ MONTES's essays and stories have appeared in journals such as *The Afro-Hispanic Review* and *Fifth Wednesday Journal,* and she regularly writes for *La Bloga,* the international Chicanx/Latinx blogsite. Montes is an associate professor in the Department of English at the University of Nebraska–Lincoln. She is finishing a memoir on her Fulbright year in the former Yugoslavia (The Ohio State University Press). An excerpt of this book was nominated for a Pushcart Prize.

COLLEEN O'CONNOR received her MFA in nonfiction from Columbia College Chicago. She is the author of the chapbooks *The Pretty Thing to Do* (Dancing Girl Press) and *Conversations with Orson* (Essay Press). Recent work has appeared in the *Atticus Review, Pinwheel,* and *Barrelhouse,* where her essay "Cautionary" was a featured novella-length essay. She lives in Chicago, where she serves as coeditor of *The Lettered Streets Press.*

JOSÉ ORDUÑA is an essayist originally from Córdoba, Veracruz, who immigrated to Chicago when he was a child. He holds an MFA from the University of Iowa's Nonfiction Writing Program, and his first book, *The Weight of Shadows: A Memoir of Immigration and Displacement,* was published by Beacon Press. His work has been anthologized and has appeared in publications such as Timothy McSweeney's *Quarterly Concern, TriQuarterly,* and the North American Congress on Latin America.

JERICHO PARMS is the author of *Lost Wax.* Her essays have appeared in *Fourth Genre, The Normal School, Hotel Amerika, American Literary Review,* and elsewhere. Her work has been nominated for the Pushcart Prize, noted in *Best American Essays,* and anthologized in *Brief Encounters: A Collection of Contemporary Nonfiction* and *Waveform: Twenty-First-Century Essays by Women.* She has an MFA from Vermont College of Fine Arts and teaches in the professional writing program at Champlain College.

JERALD WALKER is author of the memoirs *The World in Flames* and *Street Shadows.* His work has appeared in magazines such as *Creative Nonfiction, Harvard Review, River Teeth, The Missouri Review, Mother Jones,* and *The Iowa Review,* and he has been widely anthologized, including four times in *The Best American Essays.* His collection of essays, *How to Make a Slave,* will be published in 2020. Walker is a professor of creative writing at Emerson College.

NICOLE WALKER is the author of the nonfiction collections *The After-Normal: Brief, Alphabetical Essays on a Changing Planet*; *Sustainability: A Love Story*; *Where the Tiny Things Are*; *Egg*; *Micrograms*; and *Quench Your Thirst with Salt*.

XU XI 許素細 is author of fourteen books of fiction and nonfiction, most recently *This Fish Is Fowl: Essays of Being* (2019). She is faculty co-director of the International MFA in creative writing and literary translation at Vermont College of Fine Arts. An Indonesian Chinese American diehard transnational, she splits her life, unevenly, between the state of New York and the rest of the world. Follow her @xuxiwriter on Facebook, Instagram, Twitter, LinkedIn.

21st CENTURY ESSAYS
David Lazar and Patrick Madden, Series Editors

This series from Mad Creek Books is a vehicle to discover, publish, and promote some of the most daring, ingenious, and artistic nonfiction. This is the first and only major series that announces its focus on the essay—a genre whose plasticity, timelessness, popularity, and centrality to nonfiction writing make it especially important in the field of nonfiction literature. In addition to publishing the most interesting and innovative books of essays by American writers, the series publishes extraordinary international essayists and reprint works by neglected or forgotten essayists, voices that deserve to be heard, revived, and reprised. The series is a major addition to the possibilities of contemporary literary nonfiction, focusing on that central, frequently chimerical, and invariably supple form: The Essay.

---

*Annual Gournay Prize Winner

Love's Long Line
SOPHFRONIA SCOTT

The Real Life of the Parthenon
PATRICIA VIGDERMAN

You, Me, and the Violence
CATHERINE TAYLOR

Curiouser and Curiouser: Essays
NICHOLAS DELBANCO

Don't Come Back
LINA MARÍA FERREIRA CABEZA-VANEGAS

A Mother's Tale
PHILLIP LOPATE